A War of Words

Recent Titles in
Contributions in Ethnic Studies
Series Editor: Leonard W. Doob

A WAR OF WORDS

Chicano Protest in the 1960s and 1970s

John C. Hammerback,
Richard J. Jensen,
AND
Jose Angel Gutierrez

Contributions in Ethnic Studies, Number 12

GREENWOOD PRESS
WESTPORT, CONNECTICUT • LONDON, ENGLAND

1985

Library of Congress Cataloging in Publication Data

Hammerback, John C.
   A war of words.

   (Contributions in ethnic studies, ISSN 0196-7088;
no. 12)
   Bibliography: p.
   Includes index.
   1. Mexican American leadership—Politics and
government.   2. Mexican Americans—Politics and
government.   3. United States—Social conditions—
1960-   .   4. Civil rights movements—United States—
History—20th century.   5. Rhetoric—Political aspects
—United States.   6. United States—Ethnic relations.
I. Jensen, Richard J.   II. Gutierrez, Jose Angel.
III. Title.   IV. Series.
E184.M5H36   1985   323.1′16872′073   85-5598
ISBN 0-313-24825-7 (lib. bdg. : alk. paper)

Library of Congress Catalog Card Number: 85–5598
ISBN: 0-313-24825-7
ISSN: 0196-7088

First published in 1985

Greenwood Press
A division of Congressional Information Service, Inc.
88 Post Road West
Westport, Connecticut 06881

Printed in the United States of America

10 9 8 7 6 5 4 3 2 1

Copyright acknowledgments:

Grateful acknowledgment is given for permission to reprint the following:

Passages from *I Am Joaquin* by Rodolfo "Corky" Gonzales. New York: Bantam
Books, 1972. Copyright by Rodolfo Gonzales.

Contents

Series Foreword

The Contributions in Ethnic Studies series focuses on the problems that arise when people with different cultures and goals come together and interact productively or tragically. The modes of adjustment or conflict are various, but usually one group dominates or attempts to dominate the other. Eventually some accommodation is reached: the process is likely to be long and, for the weaker group, painful. No one scholarly discipline monopolizes the research necessary to comprehend these intergroup relations. The emerging analysis, consequently, is of interest to historians, social scientists, psychologists, psychiatrists, and scholars in communication studies.

The numerical, political, economic, and social importance of Mexican-Americans, generally known as Chicanos, has become self-evident not only in the Southwest and California, but also throughout the United States. In the words of a poem by one of their leaders, once these people were, and to a certain extent still are, "lost in a world of confusion/ caught up in the whirl of a gringo society/ confused by the rules/ scorned by attitudes/ suppressed by manipulation/ and destroyed by modern society." During the decades of the 1960s and the 1970s, however, their status and condition improved somewhat. *A War of Words* charts the principal reasons for the changes by examining the activities of the four principal leaders, one of whom wrote the quoted poem and another a final chapter interpreting the history and ideology of the people, as well as of five Chicano Establishment political figures in Congress. The flavor of these efforts is conveyed by the names given to two of their own organizations: the Crusade for Freedom and La Raza Unida. Chicano nationalism has made itself known not only in Mexico and other Central American countries, but also in Europe and the Middle East.

The emphasis of the volume is not on the personal lives of the leaders, though the trials and accomplishments of each are briefly sketched, but on the rhetorical discourse they "designed to induce attitudes and influence actions" of their own groups and often to shame Anglos. Following Mexican and Indian tradition, at first the rhetoric was transmitted in face-to-face encounters and reached soul-moving heights. The mass media have also been skillfully utilized. Copious quotations from the compelling speeches indicate that the leaders based the rhetoric on their interpretation of Christianity and especially on the general and specific rights supposedly possessed by all peoples. The glittering, powerful oratory, however, has been only a prelude to activities which have included political pressure, strikes, and boycotts. No American of this period can forget grapes and Cesar Chavez, and the rebels among college students of the 1960s must remember the support they received and gave to the Chicanos in the West.

These Chicano contemporaries—whether their parents or grandparents or they themselves moved into American farms and cities from south of the border—have enriched American society with their language and diverse cultural interests. This book reinforces an old theme: at first strangers may be unwelcome, but later, provided they refuse to be humiliated, provided they learn to be proud of their own heritage, and provided they make certain adaptations, they will join the rest of us and we all may rejoice. Or at least we should rejoice.

Leonard W. Doob

Acknowledgments

The authors incurred a considerable debt of gratitude during their work on this book. Special thanks to Professor Matt S. Meier, the dean of historians of the Mexican-Americans, for his detailed criticisms of the final draft of our manuscript. His comments led to the removal of faulty data and questionable interpretations. The assistance of Lynn Sedlak Flint, Maureen Melino, and other staff members at Greenwood Press further improved our finished product. The authors, of course, take full responsibility for any remaining errors. Appreciation also to Deborah Martin Brown for her aid with research on an early draft of what became the first portion of the chapter on Chavez; and to California State University, Hayward, for a small research grant and a sabbatical leave which gave John Hammerback time and money for two trips to Mexico and two to New Mexico, all necessary preparation for this book. Thanks to the Research Allocations Committee at the University of New Mexico for two small grants which helped Richard Jensen complete research for this manuscript. Of the many people who gave vital information and friendly advice, Christine Marin of the Chicano Studies Collection at the Hayden Library at Arizona State University, Chaplain Winthrop Yinger of the California Maritime Academy, and Nelly Fernandez of the Alameda County, California, library were particularly generous. Jose Angel Gutierrez wishes to add: "Dedico mi porcion de este libro a Elvirita de la Fuente, Maria L. Hernandez, Virginia Muzauiz, Olivia Serna y Pepe Hernandez."

Special thanks to May Polivka for typing early drafts of the manuscript and to Jeannie Stokes for typing the final manuscript.

Finally, one last thank you to our wives, Jean Melton Hammerback, Carol Jensen, and Luz Gutierrez, for continued spiritual support as well as assistance in typing and proofreading.

A War of Words

1

Introduction: Chicano Rhetoric

In the turbulent period of reform and protest in the 1960s and early 1970s, Mexican-American organizations and leaders implored their people to speak out for their share of the American Dream. Documents of the National Farm Workers Association and the Movimiento Estudiantil Chicano de Aztlan (MECHA), for example, demanded that "WE SHALL BE HEARD" and pledged a campaign of "speaking and communicating" with students and of "spreading the message of the movement by any media [sic] available."[1] Mexican-American writers argued that "communication, the key to social change, lies in the realm of voicing our needs in the political arena," and that "sharing in the full life in America" depends on "a voice and a force that command attention and action."[2] The inequalities suffered by the Mexican-American people, concluded historians Matt S. Meier and Feliciano Rivera, would be overcome only when "leaders successfully articulate the common aspirations of la raza."[3]

The urgent need for Mexican-Americans to speak out was not new. In 1940 George I. Sanchez, the dean of Mexican-American scholars, labeled his people the "forgotten Americans" and lamented that in early twentieth-century New Mexico they seemed to be "incapable of voicing their views and feelings" and therefore "became cannon fodder for political guns."[4] Such descriptions of reticence and powerlessness have often been applied to

Mexican-Americans wherever they formed communities in the United States. During the unsettled revolutionary period in Mexico after 1910, large numbers of Mexico's population migrated north to perform needed work in the Southwest's agriculture, mining, railroad, and manufacturing industries. However, during the Great Depression over 300,000 of them were deported to cut welfare rolls. In the 1940s racial violence against them became so intense that the Mexican government formally protested, and in 1966 the head of the U.S. Employment Opportunity Commission found Mexican-Americans to be the "most neglected, least sponsored, most orphaned major minority group in the United States."[5] Whether reticent, inarticulate, or simply unheeded, they acquired labels as the "silent" and the "forgotten" minority.[6]

By 1960 the minority was large, if not very visible or vocal. The census recorded 4 million Mexican-Americans; the 1970 figure surpassed 6 million, about 85 percent of whom lived in the Southwest (including California) where they formed some 12 percent of the population. Adding illegal immigrants to the figure would have pushed it to somewhere near 7.5 million. They were the second-largest minority in the nation, the largest in the Southwest, and the fastest growing, with the highest birthrate and lowest median age of any ethnic group. In many communities Mexican-Americans made up a majority of the population and gave it its dominant culture and language. An ethnic group probably "more diverse in social composition than any immigrant minority group in American history," it also retained much of the Mexican culture and generally stressed "different values from those emphasized in Anglo-American society."[7]

The first extensive research on Mexican-Americans appeared in the 1960s and revealed exigencies that demanded a ringing protest. There was widespread discrimination and prejudice against them in jobs, salaries, housing, education, voting rights, social organizations, civil rights, and the legal system. Evidence in the field of education, for example, indicated that Mexican-Americans faced as much discrimination in schools as did blacks, were routinely placed in vocational rather than academic programs, and were labeled mentally retarded in proportionately higher percentages because of the insensitivity of teachers and tests to their language and culture.[8]

Discrimination contributed to their economic, educational, and political deprivation. Brown Americans were "worse off in every respect than the non-whites (Negroes, Indians, and Orientals), not to mention the dominant Anglos (everybody else). They are poorer, their housing is more crowded and more dilapidated, their unemployment rate is higher, their average educational level is lower (two years below non-white, four below Anglo)."[9] In 1960 one-third of Mexican-American families in the Southwest lived below the poverty level of $3,000 a year. Even academic America mistreated citizens of Spanish or Mexican descent: historians were late in examining their history; and social scientists, ignoring the effects of history on Mexican-Americans, often confusing effect with cause, stereotyped them as fatalistic and underachieving, code words for some for lazy, passive, and unintelligent.[10]

Responding to the dissatisfaction and frustration of its people, the Chicano movement burst into public awareness in the mid-1960s. The broad movement drew energy from many new activist organizations, particularly from those of young people, who formed MECHA, the Mexican-American Youth Organization (MAYO), the Brown Berets, and other groups. As the movement formed and developed, four young activists emerged as its most prominent leaders: Cesar Chavez, Reies Lopez Tijerina, Rodolfo "Corky" Gonzales, and Jose Angel Gutierrez.[11] Adding to the feeling of newness of leadership, participation, and hope, the term *Chicano* increasingly became the symbol of self-identification for many activists. Although the term has carried different meanings to different people, and although extensive discussion and examination of its origins have been inconclusive, for many people Chicano connoted a militant stance, confrontation actions, and intense pride associated with the movement for brown identity and power.[12]

Rhetorical discourse—here defined as persuasive communication designed to induce attitudes and influence actions—formed and furthered the protest. Public address was the primary means by which Chavez, Tijerina, Gonzales, and Gutierrez became leaders as they worked their separate corners of Chicano America to develop their respective organizations and attain their goals. Each relied extensively on discourse and could not have achieved prominence or power without his impressive skill with words. Meanwhile, a dialectic between militants and moderates developed as Congressman Henry B. Gonzalez (D-Texas) and other Mexican-American political leaders laid out counter-arguments against activists in general and Gutierrez in particular.

It should be no surprise that the Chicano leaders are men of words as well as of action. First, Chicano listeners share a tradition from Spain, Greece, and the Near East of appreciating orators who employ an emotionally charged style. Second, immigrant and first-generation Mexican-Americans have had a high degree of illiteracy, perhaps accounting for the popularity of *corridos*, the folk ballads that carry so much of Chicano history and culture.[13] Finally, books have not been a "major part of either Spanish or Indian heritage. For the Mexican-American, the spoken language has been the primary means of transmitting" significant information.[14] Mexican-Americans expect, appreciate, and follow leaders who speak effectively.

Although Chicanos followed no single leader of national strategy, together the leading militant spokesmen popularized the themes, appeals, and symbols that formed a powerful vision of what the United States had been, was, and ought to be for Mexican-Americans. This vision of reality, complete with villains and heroes, pathos and logic, dramatic conflicts and suspected conspiracies, influenced attitudes and actions, not only in local audiences but also on a national level. While not synonymous with the Chicano experience, Chicano rhetoric altered perceptions of events, people, and places and organized the scattered direct and indirect experiences of individual listeners into a broad and cohesive interpretation of reality. The Chicano movement, along with the accompanying protest movements of blacks and others, lost much of its vitality and effectiveness by the middle 1970s, but the rhetorical vision it developed still orients many Mexican-Americans and their organizations. Because rhetoric functions to construct reality for listeners or readers and thereby influences their behavior, and because rhetorical discourse was an integral part of the careers of the principal Chicano leaders, the study of Chicano rhetoric is indispensable in understanding the Chicano protest movement.

When David J. Weber pointed out in 1973 that the "surface of Mexican-American history . . . has hardly been scratched," he could have added that the discourse which played so large a part in that recent history had been wholly untouched.[15] Before 1980 no books and only one article (Lloyd D. Powers, "Chicano Rhetoric: Some Basic Concepts," *Southern Speech Communication Journal*, Summer 1973) analyzed or evaluated Chicano public discourse. In contrast, the rhetorical discourse of blacks and women had stimulated the writing of numerous articles and books.

In this book we will attempt to remedy the neglect of Chicano rhetoric, continuing the work we began in 1980 in the *Western Journal of Speech Communication*.[16] We will focus our study on the four leaders of the Chicano movement and on the counter-rhetoric of other Mexican-American political leaders, demonstrating similarities as well as differences in the backgrounds, training in discourse, careers, and rhetoric of each respective leader. Each man respectively addressed different audiences on different issues in different parts of the United States, and each man's manner, style, and content of public communication reflected his own circumstances and being. Accordingly, we will use a descriptive focus and analytical approach suited to each particular rhetor in order to provide insights into the rhetoric of each man. We hope to uncover much of the why, how, and with what effect these leaders employed rhetorical discourse, and thereby to learn something of the nature, function, and meaning of the rhetoric of the Chicano movement.

John Hammerback wrote the Introduction, the chapters on Chavez and Tijerina, and the conclusion, all with assistance from Richard Jensen; Jensen wrote the chapters on Gutierrez, "Corky" Gonzales, and the other Mexican-American political leaders, all in collaboration with Hammerback. The two authors shared responsibility for the bibliographic essay. Jose Angel Gutierrez provides a path to understanding through his interpretation of Chicano history and ideology and their relationship to the movement's rhetoric. Throughout the book, the terms *Chicano* and *Mexican-American* are used interchangeably.

A final note: Authors and publishers, including many of those cited in our footnotes, have been notoriously inconsistent and occasionally incorrect in their use of accents for Spanish words.

This inconsistency creates confusion for some readers. Moreover, whether Spanish words are accented or not, those readers familiar with Spanish will be likely to know correct pronunciation while those unfamiliar will not. Therefore, we have decided not to accent Spanish words in this book.

NOTES

1. "The Plan of Delano," *El Malcriado* (Keene, Calif.), No. 31, 17 March 1966, rpt. in *Aztlan: An Anthology of Mexican-American Literature*, ed. Luis Valdez and Stan Steiner (New York: Vintage Books, 1972), p. 199; "El Plan de Santa Barbara," in *Readings on La Raza: The Twentieth Century*, ed. Matt S. Meier and Feliciano Rivera (New York: Hill and Wang, 1974), pp. 229–230.

2. Gloria Lopez McKnight, "Communication: The Key to Social Change," in *La Causa Chicana: The Movement for Justice*, ed. Margaret M. Mangold (New York: Family Service Association of America, 1971), p. 204; Y. Arturo Cabrera, *Emerging Faces: The Mexican-Americans* (Dubuque, Iowa: William C. Brown, 1971), p. 32.

3. Matt S. Meier and Feliciano Rivera, *The Chicanos: A History of Mexican-Americans* (New York: Hill and Wang, 1972), p. 280.

4. George I. Sanchez, *The Forgotten People* (Albuquerque: University of New Mexico Press, 1940), p. 18. Mexican-Americans have often been described as a forgotten or little-known minority in the United States. David J. Weber, "Introduction," *Foreigners in Their Native Land: Historical Roots of the Mexican-Americans*, ed. David J. Weber (Albuquerque: University of New Mexico Press, 1973), p. 1.

5. Franklin Delano Roosevelt, Jr., quoted in Ray Shaw, "Overlooked Minority," *Wall Street Journal*, 3 May 1966, p. 1.

6. Some observers have argued that Mexican-Americans have had a long tradition of active protests but that these protests were ignored. It was not that the "forgotten Americans" had awakened, claimed Armando G. Gutierrez and Herbert Hirsch, but that "the scholars and political authorities had awakened." "Political Maturation and Political Awareness: The Case of the Crystal City Chicano," *Aztlan: Chicano Journal of the Social Sciences and the Arts* 5 (Spring and Fall 1974), p. 295.

7. Joan W. Moore, *Mexican Americans* (Englewood Cliffs, N.J.: Prentice-Hall, 1970), p. 1.; Meier and Rivera, *The Chicanos*, pp. xvii-xviii.

8. NEA study cited in "The Invisible Minority," *Newsweek*, 29 August 1966, p. 46; "The Struggle for Chicano Liberation," *International Socialist Review* (November 1971), rpt. in "Chicano Nationalism," *Readings in La Raza*, ed. Meier and Rivera, p. 223; Moore, pp. 80–81.

9. Helen Rowan, "A Minority Nobody Knows," *The Atlantic*, June 1967, p. 47.

10. Chicanos vigorously attacked the research and thinking of such social scientists. See, for example, "Introduction," *Voices: Readings from El Grito*, ed. Octavio I. Romano V (Berkeley: Quito Sol Publications, 1971), pp. 19ff.

11. Meier and Rivera, *The Chicanos*, pp. 257–258.

12. People of Mexican and Spanish descent in the United States have preferred and still prefer various forms of self-identification, including American, Mexican-American, Chicano, Latino, and Hispano. In the 1960s the term *Chicano* gained popularity, initially as a term of self-identification for those persons who were most militant in pressing demands of the Mexican-American people, and later for many of those who wanted to maintain their Mexican or Spanish cultural heritage. For a discussion of the roots, uses, and meanings of the term *Chicano*, see F. Chris Garcia and Rudolph O. de la Garza, *The Chicano Political Experience: Three Perspectives* (North Scituate, Mass.: Duxbury Press, 1977), pp. 14–17.

13. "An Interview with Bert Corona," *Western Journal of Speech Communication* 44 (Summer 1980), pp. 214–215; Rodolfo Acuña, *Occupied America: The Chicanos' Struggle Toward Liberation* (San Francisco: Canfield Press, 1972), p. 123; Arnulfo D. Trejo, "Of Books and Libraries," *The Chicanos: As We See Ourselves*, ed. Arnulfo D. Trejo (Tucson: University of Arizona Press, 1979), p. 172.

14. Trejo, p. 172.

15. Weber, p. 8.

16. In the *Western Journal of Speech Communication* 44 (Summer 1980), see John C. Hammerback and Richard J. Jensen, "The Rhetorical Worlds of Cesar Chavez and Reies Tijerina," pp. 166–176; Richard J. Jensen and John C. Hammerback, "Radical Nationalism Among Chicanos: The Rhetoric of Jose Angel Gutierrez," pp. 191–202; John C. Hammerback, "An Interview with Bert Corona," pp. 214–220; Richard J. Jensen, "An Interview with Jose Angel Gutierrez," pp. 203–213; and Michael Victor Sedano, "Chicanismo: A Rhetorical Analysis of Themes and Images of Selected Poetry from the Chicano Movement," pp. 177–190. An article on Rodolfo Gonzales by Jensen and Hammerback is in the Winter 1982 issue of the *Western Journal of Speech Communication*, pp. 72–91.

2

"The Tongue of a Latin Moses": The Rhetoric of Reies Tijerina

In 1958 Reies Lopez Tijerina, a thirty-one-year-old itinerant Protestant minister from Texas, drifted into northern New Mexico, a predominantly rural region with the state's heaviest proportion of Spanish-speaking residents and some of its worst economic deprivation.[1] In these mountains and valleys, the inhabitants of villages and towns, which had been physically and culturally isolated for centuries, clung to many ways of the Spaniards and Mexicanos who had settled there beginning in 1598. These New Mexicans often called themselves Hispanos, a term which emphasized their Spanish lineage. Changing from Mexican to American rule after the Mexican-American War, they found themselves under an unfamiliar legal system and customs that did not recognize their prevailing Spanish custom of *ejidos*, or communal land. Falling prey to swindles, taxes, legal technicalities, and the complexities of American law, as well as changes in the policies of the National Forest Service, Spanish-speaking New Mexicans lost some 3.7 million acres of community and privately owned land and their rights to graze cattle and sheep in national forests.[2] Sociologist Clark S. Knowlton concluded that the loss of this land, the basis of the people's agrarian life, produced "a large depressed region marked by rates of disease, malnutrition, hunger, infant mortality, unemployment and welfare at least as high as similar rates among the Negroes of Mississippi."[3] By 1960 over one-half of the northern Hispanos were receiving welfare payments.[4]

As Tijerina preached to the "increasingly bitter and distrustful" village people, a people beginning to see itself as a separate race, he grew ever more excited about the issue of the lost land.[5] He traveled to Mexico on two occasions where he spent more than a year gathering information on land grants and laws. Upon returning to the north in May 1960, he launched a "virtually unabated" seven-year campaign to convince New Mexicans that centuries-old land grants guaranteed them their lost property.[6] During this "essentially . . . one-man campaign," he spoke "at meetings of land grant organizations, meetings of ditch organizations, in rented halls, in churches, wherever listeners might gather," even traveling "from house to house, speaking to the men in the fields and the women in the kitchens, preaching to the families far into the nights, exhorting the informal gatherings."[7]

In the autumn of 1961, two weeks after some Hispanos were beaten by an Anglo landowner, Tijerina addressed about 150 listeners outside a schoolhouse. He later recalled that "this was the first time there was unity. The people were aroused at the things done to them."[8] He continued to speak frequently in this promising rhetorical situation, and by the end of 1962 most Hispanos in the north knew of him and many had heard him speak.[9]

Tijerina saw a pressing need to unite Hispano land grant heirs— a group that included many of New Mexico's 300,000 Spanish-speaking residents—and their numerous, often competing organizations.[10] According to one of his biographers, Tijerina accomplished this unification through his persuasive public address, which had expanded to include daily radio talks and a newspaper column in Spanish in the widely distributed Albuquerque *News Chieftain*.[11] In 1963 Tijerina founded the Alianza Federal de los Mercedes, his unifying organization, and began an extensive canvass for members. To gather information on land grants, he traveled as far as Spain to research old records. From 1963 through 1965 Alianza meetings attracted mostly the rural poor; in 1966 growing numbers of urban as well as rural poor heard Tijerina deliver his basic message at meetings.[12] The Alianza grew rapidly to between 10,000 and 15,000 members, with most new members brought in "through the personal charisma and dynamic speaking ability of Tijerina."[13] Alianza finances also relied on Tijerina's public address, for as Richard Gardner reported: "All of Tijerina's lieutenants acknowledged that only Reies could get appreciable amounts of money out of members and that it had to be done in person, preferably with a moderate-sized crowd upon which he could work the magic of his speaking style."[14] Rounding out his multimedia campaign, Tijerina began television addresses in November 1965.[15]

Expanding his message and his prominence in the middle 1960s, Tijerina called for cultural, economic, political, and educational rights for all Mexican-Americans, and he led mass-action demonstrations and an illegal occupation of a national forest campground. When armed Alianza members seized and shot up the county court house in Tierra Amarilla in an attempt at a citizen's arrest of an unfriendly district attorney, Tijerina catapulted into international notoriety.[16] As National Guardsmen mobilized tanks and artillery in the ensuing search for Alianzists, the soldiers repeatedly talked of "Tijerina, whose gift is voice and gesture; who it is felt, might be capable of inciting a full-scale revolution."[17] Although some evidence indicated that Tijerina had led the violent takeover, he later won acquittal—and expanded his reputation as a skilled orator—after pleading his own case during the trial.

After the raid Tijerina was a celebrity among American activists. He shared the speaking platform with black militants such as Ron Karenga and Ralph Featherstone, conferred with Martin Luther King, Jr., lectured to audiences in Chicago at the National Conference for New Politics, headed New Mexico's contingent at Resurrection City during the Poor People's Campaign, and addressed audiences at college campuses and other locations through the Southwest and California.[18] A hero to such militant Chicano groups as the Brown Berets,[19] he received favorable coverage in radical publications such as the Los Angeles *Free Press* (10–17 November 1967) and The Student Non-Violent Coordinating Committee's *The Movement* (August 1967). Continuing to be newsworthy, he led a series of attempts at citizens' arrests of government officials, including Chief Justice Warren Burger and the governor of New Mexico, David Cargo.[20]

Although popular among many members of the Mexican-American community, Tijerina drew vitriolic attacks from moderate and conservative sources. New Mexican Senator Joseph Montoya labeled him "a damned liar, an enemy of the United States, . . . impostor, racist and creature of darkness"; the John Birch Society and other right-wing sources accused him of being a Communist, or worse.[21] Expressing the sentiments of many of Tijerina's critics, a police agent who had Tijerina under surveillance for three years warned that, although he had seen Tijerina commit no act of violence, "every time he opens his mouth it's violent. He goes up north and spreads his crap around—I can't understand why he isn't in jail."[22] Meanwhile, in 1968 *Newsweek* pointed out that growing numbers of "frustrated Mexican-Americans have been rallying to the banner" of Tijerina.[23]

The growth of Tijerina's movement stopped in June 1969, when he went to prison for violating his parole connected with earlier charges resulting from his seizure of federal property. By this time the controversial spokesman had become "a hero and the very symbol of the hopes and aspirations of militant young Mexican-American and Spanish-American groups from Los Angeles to San Antonio."[24] When he was paroled two years later, he shifted his message to human brotherhood and lost his leadership in the Chicano movement. As part of his parole he could not hold a position in the movement.

Tijerina's public address earned him recognition as "undoubtedly the most charismatic of the Chicano leaders," "a fiery spellbinder" who among the Southwest's poor had "the drawing power and persuasive tongue of a Latin Moses."[25] Although biographers and scholars chronicled his life and explained his movement as a nativist cult or a civil rights movement, Tijerina received no in-depth rhetorical study, nor has the public address which created and built his organization from 1960 to 1965 been examined.[26] This chapter will focus on his rhetorical crusade in New Mexico, identifying two biographical elements crucial to his success and analyzing his rhetorical message during the years from 1963 to 1965.

TIJERINA'S BACKGROUND

Tijerina possessed the ideal background for his life as a spokesman for New Mexicans. Able to share experiences with Hispanos who suffered discrimination and poverty, he had grown up in the deprived world of migrant farmworkers and sharecroppers and had suffered as his father was cheated by Anglo landowners. Although his family's penniless, wandering life allowed him no more than a total of six months of formal education, young Reies possessed natural rhetorical gifts. "Right from my childhood," he recalled, "I was distinguished in the art of persuasion. They called me *abogado sin libros*, 'lawyer without books.' "[27]

In his mid-teens he received a New Testament from a Baptist minister, read it, and found new direction for his life. At the age of nineteen he entered an Assembly of God Bible college in Ysleta, Texas, studied there for three years, and then began preaching in Victoria, Texas. Although he earned a reputation as a fiery and effective speaker from the pulpit, disagreements with officials of the church cost Tijerina his minister's credentials in 1950. He spent most of the next decade as an itinerant preacher of fundamentalist Christianity, addressing congregations in tents, halls, and churches mainly in the Southwest, South, and California. After an unsuccessful attempt in the mid-1950s to establish a utopian religious commune in Arizona, Tijerina moved to New Mexico and discovered audiences of Christians who seemed to be more concerned with regaining their land than with securing their souls.[28]

Tijerina remembers his years as a traveling preacher as a "training period."[29] By 1958 he had developed into a charismatic communicator for Christ. Richard Gardner described him as being at that time

a solidly built man in his early thirties, with thick black hair and glinting gray-green eyes, a personal presence which seemed forever on the brink of some cataclysmic ecstasy and a speaking style that would compel the most skeptical sheepherder to come forward with at least a dollar in his hand and his eyes agleam with a yearning for instant transmutation from damned to delivered, from lost to found.[30]

His evangelist's vibrant presence and dynamic manner of delivering speeches remained with him through the next decade.

Tijerina's experience using the Bible's rich imagery, vivid illustrations, and deep moral sentiments to persuade Spanish-speaking congregations also influenced his public address of the

1960s. The four authors of books on Tijerina in the 1960s called attention to his preacher's preference for figurative language, allusions, and parables, reporting, respectively, that his ideas, like those in the Bible, were largely explained through parable; that "he spices his rhetoric with biblical references" which are "the allusions most familiar to his listeners"; that he lashed his audiences "with the staccato rhythms of his preacher's voice, goading them with a mind gifted with metaphor and trained to the single, compelling phrase"; and that his speaking was "a masterly, exhausting exhibition of folk rhetoric, savage mimicry, lapses into his backlog of fundamentalist fables, and an actor's shifting of emotional levels."[31]

Tijerina's background identified him with his audiences, and his experience as an orator prepared him well to speak to Hispanos, but these elements alone do not explain his persistent campaign in the face of obstacles that would have discouraged even the most skilled speaker. He strove to lead a group which lacked money, power, and education, and he himself lacked these means to lead successfully. Although his first audiences were unresponsive, and one gathering of rural New Mexicans even bloodied his head in a brawl following his speech, he continued to canvass widely.[32] Tijerina's unflagging advocacy, especially during these first years in New Mexico, is as remarkable as his rhetorical skill.

TIJERINA'S MOTIVATION AS AN ORATOR

Tijerina's motivation to persuade came largely from his view of God's plan for him. Born into a Roman Catholic family, he accepted the orthodox Christian view that God can control events on earth. Unlike many Christians, however, Tijerina claimed to receive divine blueprints for the future. At the age of four he had a dream that Christ led him by the hand to a beautiful country. After a later dream in which God called him to lead Mexican-Americans out of bondage, he enrolled in Bible school to prepare to lead his people.[33] In still another dream, this one during a solitary retreat to pray in the hills of California, he saw tall pines, frozen horses, and three angels, a vision he interpreted to mean that old, obscure laws would be thawed to allow

New Mexicans to regain the high northern land which had been rightfully deeded to them by land grants.[34]

During the 1960s he concluded that it was not a historical accident that Spaniards colonized much of the New World. The merging of Spaniards and Indians was God's design for a brown race which would eventually lead older and morally decaying races to a millennial order of peace and happiness.[35] Tijerina called his new race a "new breed," one only 450 years old.[36] This new breed, he asserted, possessed the moral values, typified by love of God and family, that would satisfy the world's hunger for moral order.[37] Southwestern Hispanos, Tijerina decided, would serve as a vital link to Latin America and simultaneously bring together bickering blacks and whites in the United States. He often exhorted his listeners to build a new order, a new world.[38]

Tijerina saw himself as the shepherd whom God had chosen to guide Hispanos toward their divine destiny. He identified with Moses, who had led an oppressed people to the promised land. Aligning himself with other biblical leaders, Tijerina disclosed: "My rebukes against the United States are just the same as those rebukes of the prophets. . . . There is no hate included. I would just like to see this nation converted to God, repent and improve relations with other nations."[39]

As an agent in God's plan, Tijerina was swept along by a force for justice which he saw as, "more powerful than any nation, than the United States, than anything."[40] Revealing the relationship between himself and this force, he claimed in 1968: "The cause of justice in New Mexico depends on my reputation."[41] On another occasion he confided: "I am a symbol. I can't help it, I didn't mean it this way, but it's true. It is bigger than me, this demand for justice."[42] He summarized his place in God's plan: "Our people had not a guide, no light, no knowledge, and God therefore has chosen me."[43]

Public address was Tijerina's means to God's ends. Convinced throughout his life that he had a natural gift for oratory,[44] he relied on this gift to present the case for Hispanic rights to ownership of land and later for many other rights. He sought to expand his persuasive potential in many ways. He learned English because of his desire to reach broader audiences; rejoined the Catholic Church because he was certain that "his people expect it"; and, after an earlier marriage failed, married a fifteen-year-old land claimant because he believed it necessary to show his followers that he had a real interest in the land issues.[45] Displaying a distinctly rhetorical orientation to the workings of the world, he lectured various audiences on the importance of shifting the "burden of proof" from the poor to the rich, from Hispanos to the government.[46] In Tijerina's mind, the battle with government was simply "a war of words, of law, of interpretation."[47]

His religious beliefs merged with his political message. When Tijerina announced his third-party candidacy for governor in 1968, he told an audience not to be discouraged, because "We can believe in a miracle."[48] He interpreted the bloody takeover at Tierra Amarilla in this manner: "We don't believe in violence, but we believe in Jesus Christ. The revolution at Tierra Amarilla was like Christ entering the temple and cleaning out the Pharisees."[49] An extension of its leader, the Alianza was unique in the Chicano movement "in its strong emotional religious flavor and a deep feeling of millennial purpose."[50] Because he viewed his rhetorical crusade as a crucial part of God's plan and therefore expected success regardless of temporary setbacks, it is not so surprising that he devoted his life to campaigning for his seemingly hopeless cause.

TIJERINA'S PUBLIC ADDRESS

The rhetorical message which created Tijerina's grass-roots support contained two major substantive themes: Anglos had illegally taken the Hispanos' land in northern New Mexico and throughout the Southwest; and the law would remedy the injustice if Hispanos' presented their case effectively. This message dominated his articles for the Albuquerque *News Chieftain* from 1963 to January 1966, the only extant remnants of his rhetorical magic during that period.[51]

On 7 June 1963, Tijerina's first essay told readers of the "plunder of more than two million square kilometers of our territory" through the Mexican-American War.[52] After the war Mexico and the United States promised "protection to the thousands and thousands of Mexicans" in the new U.S. territory, but the "North American government fell short of its word, as always." Instead of protecting the conquered Mexicans, the government "invaded their rights, confiscated their properties, and did not recognize their legal existence." In subsequent articles Tijerina underscored the central theme that the land had been illegally confiscated, sometimes citing specific cases such as the Merced de Tierra Amarilla in which 594,000 acres were "stolen" by "foreigners."[53]

In October 1963 Tijerina proudly named forty-two Hispanos who claimed to be heirs and had joined the Alianza; he urged others to register with him. He pointed out that New Mexico's Constitution cited the Treaty of Guadalupe Hidalgo as guaranteeing rights to land heirs and that Article 6 of the U.S. Constitution made treaties "THE SUPREME LAW OF THE LAND." Because the treaty and the property titles left to heirs by the "crown of Spain and Mexico are of the best that there are in the world," no cause on the American continent is "more legal, more justifiable, more documented than the cause of the real heirs of the real Mercedes."[54] By February of 1964 Tijerina had recruited eighty heirs and forecast that if the unification and the dues of one dollar per month continued, "soon we shall see our lands free."[55]

In April 1964 Tijerina decided that the heirs needed more details on the various laws. He cited Ordinance 99 given by King Phillip II of Spain in the *Laws of the Indias*, Book 4, Title 6, Law 6, which made *mercedes-holders* "noblemen" whose lands were protected by Spanish law later upheld by the Treaty of Guadalupe Hidalgo. The heirs' protected rights were "more valuable than any economic or political rights"; he said he would argue the validity of those laws before the U.S. government and thereby regain the lost land. Meanwhile, each heir must memorize Ordinance 99, for "if we do not recognize that they [the laws] protect our rights to our property, how are we going to defend ourselves against the judges who violate human rights? . . . I am certain that justice will prevail for the heirs," he forecast optimistically, "and that they will attend to us when they see all our people united asking for the same sacred thing."[56] In October 1964, continuing to show his faith in legal redress, he disclosed that "the biggest and most important document that the history of New Mexico has ever known is being prepared." This petition to the U.S. Senate, and thus to the "whole inhabited world," would be signed by all 120 Alianza registrants and would present the truth of the frauds and illegal laws which deprived heirs of "THE RIGHTS, PRIVILEGES, AND THE MATERIAL AND PERSONAL ITEMS" guaranteed by "LAWS OF THE INDIAS through the Treaty of Guadalupe Hidalgo, and by the Federal Constitution of the United States."[57]

In the summer of 1965, after "ninety consecutive days" of radio speeches about property rights, Tijerina warned that further claims would be received only until 4 and 6 September 1965. "We have told all of the heirs plenty of times," he reminded readers, "inviting and begging" them to record their claims.[58] As 1965 ended, he declared that throughout his "eight long years" of investigating the history of the *mercedes*, he had remained convinced that justice would be secured.[59] When it appeared that the heirs could take their case to the Supreme Court, he boasted: "If the Alianza Federal had not been born yet we would be far from seeing justice done. But now that all of the town heirs of the Mercedes have united, we feel that soon we will get justice."[60]

The goal of justice, he tirelessly repeated, depended on the effective presentation of the Hispano's case. Early in his crusade he lamented that the "cry of the people has never arrived at the ears of the Federal Government." Promising to "publish all of the injustices . . . so that all will come to know and realize" the suffering of the heirs, he predicted that the crimes against them soon "will come out in the light of the world and the guilty evil ones will be punished."[61] "It is our turn to ask for justice," he later contended, "and if we ask for it united we shall soon reach it."[62]

Tijerina sought to discover and disseminate the information and arguments necessary to persuade. He asked heirs for facts to bolster his own research, and he published statistics on acres stolen and people displaced, examples of land plunder, quotes of reporters and politicians, and citations from actual laws.[63] Heirs were instructed to become familiar with the evidence and thus to become persuasive communicators themselves.

Tijerina began to seek a more prestigious and powerful audience to adjudicate his case. He spoke with the district's attorney general in Albuquerque and found encouragement that that office "for the first time admitted that the cause of the heirs was true"; addressed the department head of the Federal Farm Home Administrators and was assured that "without a doubt . . . Justice would give us our land very soon"; and was certain that three Hispanic congressmen would arrange for him to interview President Kennedy.[64] In early 1964 he traveled to Mexico to present his case to governmental officials, who "stretched their hands out to us and have promised to back us in our favor."[65] Next he planned a trip to Washington, D.C., to talk with the Secretary of the Interior, the Secretary-General of the United Nations, and the U.S. President.[66] When these audiences failed either to receive him or to resolve his claims, he called for a "great international caravan" to Mexico in the "biggest and most historical event that the founders of the Mercedes have made until this present day"—one to be "written in the history of New Mexico, Texas, California, Colorado, Arizona, Utah, and Nevada forever." "Every one of the caravaners," he asserted, "will be a personal protest and a live protest in front of the whole world; and this will be the protest that nobody will be able to silence or ignore." Because "all of the papers in the world will publicize" the caravan, everyone "will know and become convinced" of the heirs' just case.[67] Later, it was a petition to Congress which would fall "like a live bombshell," so that for "the first time in the history of the United States, the FORGOTTEN PEOPLE will present their true complaint" and "the world and the impartial courts" will know the truth. "The entire world's eyes will focus on the Congress of the United States when we present our petition," Tijerina stated, and he would address public opinion— the "true and great jury with which nobody can play."[68]

Although Tijerina proclaimed to trust the facts of his message, he developed a psychological climate conducive to accepting his themes by appealing to three animating values of Hispanos: kinship to family, community, and race; manhood; and God.[69] Appealing to kinship, he called on "the real heirs to unite and become one body or a real family, to recover everything that belongs to our sons."[70] On various occasions he declared: each must participate "in this SACRED CRUSADE for the land of our beloved sons"; "Remember, this struggle is for your land and for your children"; and protestors "will also win the appreciation of our sons."[71] The concept of family was extended to the entire race when he argued that Hispanos constituted a superior new breed of people.[72]

The Hispano was contrasted sharply to the Anglo, frequently labeled the "foreigner" (*el extranjero*) or "stranger" (*el forastero*). The "foreigner has illegally taken control of your lands," he informed, and these "guilty evil ones will be punished."[73] These foreigners are bribing officials to block the Alianza's claims and are using "lies," "violence," and "everything bad to destroy the Alianza."[74] Relating outsiders to Hispanos, he charged: "We are tired of seeing the strangers come and do what they do to our properties. We are tired of seeing our sons and daughters mistreated."[75]

Appeals to kinship sometimes merged with appeals to manliness. Those not helping to regain the land and rights plundered by strangers "do not love their race" and "will end up feeling very ashamed."[76] In contrast were the "vigorous and brave" of Tijerina's movement, men who will gain "honor and respect."[77] Caravaners to Mexico, for example, would be assured that "neither history nor our sons will ever say that we were afraid and cowardly."[78]

Tijerina's ultimate appeal invoked the deity. The Alianza should give thanks for their triumphs "to the heavens and to He who directs the destiny of our people."[79] When he failed to reach his goals, Tijerina warned that "God is tired of seeing the organized robbings that are made against our brothers. . . . He is moving us so that we can do our part."[80] It was God who was "unifying our people and . . . confusing" the enemies. He revealed the full influence of God in his movement: "Let us not forget that God is our pilot, and that He is steering the destiny of our lives like a new people."[81]

Tijerina further energized his persuasion through stylistic techniques, particularly imagery and parallelism. He spun out vivid pictures such as these: "The wicked that rob the people, and twist the laws to torture and grind the flesh of the just"; their sons and history "will say that the caravaners broke the silence of our cause and melted our rights that the strangers froze"; and, "the BLACK LEGEND fermented the hate of the Anglo against the Spanish, and the first, seeing us orphans abandoned, discharged over our fathers the vengeance and hate accumulated for 200 and more years."[82] His most common parallel construction employed simple restatement and repetition. In one essay, for example, four consecutive sentences began with, "we are tired" of various outrages against Hispanos; two sentences later he initiated two consecutive sentences with "God is tired" of particular crimes against His people. Another essay opened with "for eight long years"; the next clause with "for eight years"; and the following clause with "In those eight years." In still another essay he began a paragraph with, "We are the people," and then added six consecutive sentences or clauses beginning with "we are" or "nor are we."[83] Sometimes he compressed his parallelism within a sentence: for example, "Day by day, hour by hour, month by month, and year by year we worked"; or, "The legitimate sons and heirs that love Justice will always separate from the Judases that love the fraud and the lie."[84]

Tijerina's oral delivery was as powerful as his language. Virtually every close observer was impressed with the energy, expressiveness, and effectiveness of his voice and body. Rhetorical critic Gordon R. Owen declared: "Tijerina's sturdy physique and unusually mobile face framed by coal black hair, combined with a tremendous range of vocal pitch and intensity, enable him to hold audiences spellbound for hours." "His hands and arms," Owen continued, "move constantly, fisting, clapping, wringing, waving, flying into the air."[85] Biographer Michael Jenkinson reported: "His full-gestured delivery resembles the alternately soft and brutal histrionics of a grassroots evangelist, as indeed, he once was."[86] Stan Steiner described Tijerina speaking in a small village:

He does not make a speech; he enacts the history of the village. He performs all the roles in the historical pageant he recites. He is the lawyer, judge, victim, preacher, sufferer, farmer, oracle, avenger, and holy prophet. When he performs the ritual that everyone knows by heart he embodies all the voices, in falsetto, in basso, in *sotto voce*, in heroics, in anguish, in English, in Spanish; for he suffers the history of La Raza for everyone in the audience, as they have always told it themselves.[87]

   While Tijerina's rhetorical substance and manner remained consistent from 1963 to 1965, a tone of self-pity and desperation emerged as he failed to regain land. By 7 July 1965, he told of doing "everything within our reach, with a thousand sacrifices," to talk to Hispanos; "for three years now we have been inviting and begging all of the heirs." On 3 December, he recalled that through "eight long years" of investigating the history of the *mercedes*, the pioneers "have fought pain and a thousand obstacles and difficulties. . . . In those eight years, few know how much we have suffered." "His enemies wish him dead," he revealed; "I wish that the people would become more awake and feel the true price and cost of the mercedes." One week later he warned: "Everyday the people get more restless and more desperate; and now it cannot be contained."
   In the last half of the 1960s, Tijerina added new themes such as the coming dominance of the New Breed, the mistake of the Vietnam War, and the nobility of black militancy.[88] These themes contrasted with his ongoing conservative message of using laws to protect property rights; but of course by this time he was a celebrity among America's radicals and addressed an audience far expanded from rural New Mexico. Always sensitive to exigencies in his audience that called for a fitting rhetorical response, he linked the New Left themes in his rhetoric to the fact that "the time is coming, our time, I can feel it in me, like a natural force. The world is hungry, and the people are beginning to cry out. There is a change, a fever, and pretty soon they are going to start trampling on top of others and not caring a hoot about regulations or methods."[89] When asked if he had changed after attending a Chicago convention on New Politics, he replied: "It's not me, it's the times."[90] His views of land and justice would "come later," he added, for "there is no time for that now. Things are moving too fast."[91] Thus, whether Tijerina sought appreciation from Hispanos in 1965 or applause from radicals in 1969, he was revealing that his fundamental nature was that of a persuader rather than an ideologue.

SUMMARY AND CONCLUSIONS

Tijerina's vivid depiction of past injustice, present deprivation, and future triumphs articulated and intensified the thoughts, feelings, and experiences of his rural listeners. An essentially conservative and traditional people, his Spanish-speaking audience identified with his conservative legal principles and emphasis on family, race, religion, manliness, and glorious Spanish tradition. His authoritative historical accounts and electric style and delivery also fit the listeners' expectations. Hispanos have traditionally followed patron-leaders whose authority is powerful and action is benevolent.[92] Among his rural listeners, moreover, prophecies of a messianic leader who would lead the local landless from bondage had recurred for generations.[93]

Thus, Tijerina satisfied his listeners' inchoate dreams of a golden-tongued Spanish-speaking leader of the landless. Revealing the effect of these fulfilled expectations, a Mexican reporter who toured Hispanic villages in northern New Mexico described the near idolatry for Tijerina, whom villagers saw as the "incarnation of the justice denied them for one hundred years."[94] Another Mexican captured Tijerina's relationship with his audience: "From among them has arisen a leader, a sort of apostle of the cause of Mexican-Americans, the symbolic man in whom the ideals of the people are embodied."[95]

This study of Tijerina suggests a rhetorical model which may fit other Spanish-speaking leaders who have used public address to develop and maintain a base of power from rural listeners. Rhetorical discourse created, extended, and intensified the perceived reality of discontented people; this reality built an audience capable of action. Only through such discourse could a penniless, non-Catholic Texan gain leadership of the clannish New Mexican Catholics. Tijerina is better explained as an itinerant orator seeking an audience than as an ideologue possessing a cause.

For a time Tijerina's faith in his righteous rhetoric appeared to be warranted. He believed that his New Mexican listeners had been "ripe" for his ideas and that his audiences "got the message; . . . it was time for it."[96] When he entered New Mexico, he recalled, heirs were fearful; but because of his several years of "teaching the people," they became "lions and tigers" who overcame "their fears and terror and that sense of subordination."[97]

As the Alianza grew, "from nothing" according to one of his bitterest enemies, it became the "first movement with civil rights implications to attract attention within the state of New Mexico" and one of the first two successful Mexican-American protest movements in the United States.[98] Knowlton argues that the Alianza had "decisively broken through the apathy and hopelessness of Spanish Americans" in New Mexico; Professor Nancie L. Gonzalez calls the growth of New Mexico activism from 1966 to 1969 "remarkable"—a growth that must be attributed partly to Tijerina, New Mexico's only prominent activist during that period.[99] Discussing Tijerina's national influence, one author depicted him as the "detonator" of the explosion of national awareness of discrimination and misery suffered by Mexican-Americans.[100]

Tijerina's effects were no mere inevitable result of the confluence of historical forces in New Mexico and the United States in the turbulent 1960s. His extensive early practice of public address had trained him well to motivate and persuade Spanish-speaking listeners and had developed much of the style, delivery, and even some of the themes he would employ in the 1960s. Moreover, his view of God's plan for him and the world created and sustained his motivation to speak despite the initially long odds against success. Without his background and unusual training, skills, and attitudes as an orator, and without his rhetorically powerful combination of themes and appeals, the ripe rhetorical situation in New Mexico would likely have decayed in the absence of the unity and action of an audience mobilized by Tijerina's fitting response.[101]

NOTES

1. Richard Gardner, *!Grito! Reies Tijerina and the New Mexico Land Grant War of 1967* (Indianapolis: Bobbs-Merrill, 1970), p. 67; Peter Nabokov, *Tijerina and the Courthouse Raid* (Albuquerque: University of New Mexico Press, 1969), pp. 40–41.

2. Norma P. Herring, "Reies Lopez Tijerina: Don Quixote of New

Mexico," in *Pain and Promise: The Chicano Today*, ed. Edward Simmen, (New York: Mentor Books, 1972), p. 287; Clark S. Knowlton, "The New Mexican Land War," *The Nation*, 17 June 1968, in Simmen, pp. 259–260. New Mexico's Spanish-Americans are discussed at length in Nancie L. Gonzalez, *The Spanish-Americans of New Mexico*, rev. ed. (Albuquerque: University of New Mexico Press, 1969).

3. Knowlton, pp. 259–260.

4. Herring, p. 288.

5. Clark S. Knowlton, *New York Times*, 16 July 1967, p. vi-20, quoted in Gordon R. Owen, "Old Activists Never Die—They Just Mellow," unpublished manuscript, Speech Department, New Mexico State University, p. 17. For accounts of Tijerina's arrival in northern New Mexico and conversion to activism on the land issue, see Patricia Bell Blawis, *Tijerina and the Land Grants* (New York: International Publishers, 1971), p. 33; Gardner, pp. 67–68 and 92–93; and Nabokov, pp. 204–205 and 208–210.

6. Nabokov, pp. 204–205; Gardner, pp. 92–93.

7. Gardner, p. 92. See also Nabokov, pp. 210–211.

8. Michael Jenkinson, *Tijerina* (Albuquerque: Paisano Press, 1968), p. 57.

9. Gardner, p. 94.

10. Blawis, pp. 36 and 47–48; Jenkinson, pp. 50–51.

11. Blawis, p. 36. Tijerina explained his point of view on his daily program for two years on KABQ. Later, in 1963 or 1964, he began a daily ten-minute show on KARA. Blawis, p. 36; Nabokov, p. 215.

12. Knowlton, "The New Mexican Land War," pp. 261–262.

13. Gardner, p. 92; Gonzalez, p. 97. Estimates of the Alianza's secret membership varied greatly, with *Newsweek*'s ("Brown Power," 25 March 1969, p. 37) figure of about 14,000 as perhaps the most common. Estimates of 14,000 and 15,000 in 1965 and 1966 are in the Denver *Post* and the San Diego *Independent*, cited in Gardner, p. 119. Gonzalez (p. 97) estimates its membership in 1967 as about 10,000.

14. Gardner, p. 120.

15. Tijerina announced that his weekly television program would debut on the first Saturday of November 1965. "La Alianza Federal de Mercedes Informa," (Albuquerque) *News Chieftain*, 29 October 1965.

16. Tijerina's activities in the mid-1960s are described in Gardner, pp. 99ff; and in Nabokov, pp. 201–203.

17. Cited in Jenkinson, p. 17.

18. Nabokov, pp. 183–184, 219–225, and 240–248.

19. Ruth S. Lamb, *Mexican Americans: Sons of the Southwest* (Claremont, Calif.: Ocelot Press, 1970), p. 125.

20. "Unbelievable But Serious," Albuquerque *Journal*, 10 June 1969.

21. Senator Joseph M. Montoya quoted in Gardner, p. 235; Frances L. Swadesh, "The Alianza Movement of New Mexico," in *Minorities and Politics*, ed. Henry J. Tobias and Charles E. Woodhouse (Albuquerque: University of New Mexico Press, 1969), pp. 77–79. Nabokov (p. 20) points out that for many years Tijerina had been accused of being a Communist.

22. Quoted in Albuquerque *Tribune*, 17 June 1969; quoted in Blawis, p. 166.

23. "Brown Power," p. 37.

24. Knowlton, "The New Mexican Land War," p. 269.

25. Rodolfo Acuña, *Occupied America: The Chicano's Struggle Toward Liberation* (San Francisco: Canfield Press, 1972), p. 237; "Brown Power," p. 37; Bob Haber, "Verdict Strengthens Tijerina Movement," Denver *Post*, 29 December 1968. Many scholars have labeled Tijerina charismatic. For examples, see Joseph L. Love, "La Raza: Mexican Americans in Rebellion," *Transaction* (February 1969), in Simmen, p. 275; Matt S. Meier and Feliciano Rivera, *The Chicanos: A History of Mexican-Americans* (New York: Hill and Wang, 1972), p. 271; Gonzalez, p. 185.

26. The four biographies of Tijerina are by Blawis, Gardner, Jenkinson, and Nabokov. Explanations of the appeal and workings of the Alianza are in Peter Nabokov, "Reflections on the Alianza," *New Mexico Quarterly* 37 (Winter 1968), pp. 343–356; Love, pp. 271–285; Swadesh, pp. 53–84; and Gonzalez, pp. 93–106. The only studies of Tijerina as orator are by Owen, who views Tijerina's speeches after Tierra Amarilla and claims wrongly that Tijerina did not advocate Alianza claims before July 1966; and by John C. Hammerback and Richard J. Jensen, who examine Tijerina's motivations and preparation, but not his discourse, in "The Rhetorical Worlds of Cesar Chavez and Reies Tijerina," *Western Journal of Speech Communication* 44 (Summer 1980), pp. 166–176.

27. Quoted in Nabokov, p. 197. Tijerina's early life is chronicled in Gardner, pp. 31–38; Jenkinson, pp. 17–20; and Nabokov, pp. 193–198.

28. Gardner, pp. 38–47; Jenkinson, pp. 21–23; and Nabokov, pp. 34 and 198–204.

29. Tijerina quoted in Jenkinson, p. 21.

30. Ibid., p. 30.

31. Jenkinson, p. 55; Blawis, p. 34; Gardner, p. 93; and Nabokov, p. 212.

32. Jacqueline Bernard, *Voices of the Southwest* (New York: Firebird Books, 1972), p. 91; Jenkinson, pp. 50–51.

33. Jenkinson, p. 20; Clark S. Knowlton, "Tijerina: Hero of the Militants," *The Texas Observer*, 28 March 1969.

34. Gardner, pp. 47 and 84.

35. Tijerina interview in George W. Grayson, Jr., "Tijerina: The Evolution of a Primitive Rebel," *Commonweal* 86 (July 1967), pp. 465–466; audiotape of Tijerina interview with Richard Gardner, 8 September 1968, Peter Nabokov Papers, Zimmerman Library, University of New Mexico.

36. Tijerina speech at Saint John's College, Santa Fe, New Mexico, quoted in "Tijerina Charges U.S. Is Murdering Women, Children," Santa Fe *New Mexican*, 1 October 1967.

37. Tijerina interview with Gardner, Nabokov Papers.

38. Tijerina, on "News Parade," radio channel 9, Washington, D.C., quoted in Blawis, p. 139; Gardner, p. 131.

39. Tijerina quoted in Grayson, p. 466; Tijerina quoted in Pete Herrera and V. B. Price, "Alianza Meet Climaxed by Bomb Scare," Albuquerque *Tribune*, 23 October 1967.

40. Quoted in Gardner, p. 204.

41. Audiotape of Tijerina interview with Michael Jenkinson, 16 August 1968, Nabokov Papers.

42. Quoted in Gardner, p. 254.

43. Quoted in Santa Fe *New Mexican*, 14 June 1966, in Owen, p. 27.

44. Tijerina in telephone interview with John C. Hammerback, Albuquerque, 30 September 1975.

45. Blawis, p. 158; Tijerina cited in Gardner, pp. 255–256.

46. Tijerina speech in Albuquerque, 20 July 1968, quoted in Blawis, p. 145; Tijerina speech in Denver, quoted in Peter M. Kelley, "Spanish Heirs Seek Validation of Grants," Denver *Post*, 25 April 1966.

47. Tijerina quoted in "Cargo," Santa Fe *New Mexican*, 23 April 1967.

48. Quoted in "Reies Tijerina Enters N. M. Governor's Race," Albuquerque *Journal*, 28 July 1968.

49. Quoted in "Day of Triumph in Tierra Amarilla," Espanola, New Mexico *El Grito del Norte*, 11 January 1969.

50. Meier and Rivera, p. 270.

51. The *News Chieftain* is housed in the main branch of the Albuquerque Public Library. All articles are written in Spanish. Spelling and grammatical errors have been corrected in our English translation.

52. "One Million Mexicans Are Victims of the Yankee 'Justice.' "

53. "Violation of the Treaty of Guadalupe Hidalgo," 23 August 1963.

54. "The Alianza Federal de Mercedes Informs," 26 October 1963. Tijerina's subsequent articles carry this same title.

55. 21 February 1964.

56. 17 April 1964.

57. 9 October 1964.

58. 7 July 1965.

59. 3 December 1965.

60. 10 December 1965.

61. 23 August 1963.

62. 21 February 1964.

63. See, for examples, articles of 26 October 1963, 26 July 1963, and 7 June 1963.

64. 26 October 1963; 29 November 1963.

65. 21 February 1964.

66. 17 April 1964.

67. 22 May 1964.

68. 9 October 1964.

69. Gonzalez (pp. 59–75) discusses the importance of kinship to Hispanos. Knowlton (interview with John C. Hammerback, 23 August 1975, San Francisco) cited manhood, family, and religion as the dominant values of rural Hispanos in New Mexico. These three values have been linked consistently to Mexican-Americans by scholars who study the ethnic group.

70. 26 October 1963.

71. 26 October 1963; 29 November 1963; 22 May 1964.

72. 27 November 1964.

73. 23 August 1963.

74. 9 October 1964; 3 December 1965.

75. 10 December 1965.

76. 29 October 1963.

77. 10 December 1965; 24 December 1965.

78. 22 May 1964.

79. 9 October 1964.

80. 10 December 1965.

81. 24 December 1965.

82. 23 August 1963; 22 May 1964; 27 November 1964.

83. 10 December 1964; 3 December 1964; 27 November 1964.

84. 3 December 1965; 29 October 1965.

85. Owen, p. 31.

86. Ibid., p. 9.

87. Stan Steiner, *La Raza: The Mexican Americans* (New York: Harper and Row, 1969), p. 64.

88. These themes and others are reported in Jenkinson, p. 9; Gardner, pp. 198–199 and 208; Blawis, pp. 73–75; and are expressed in Tijerina's speeches as they appear in various newspapers of the period and in the full text of his speech at the University of Colorado, Denver, 20 November 1967, in Robert Tice, "The Rhetoric of La Raza" (unpub-

lished manuscript, 1971, Chicano Studies Collection, Hayden Library, Arizona State University).

89. Quoted in Gardner, p. 215.

90. Ibid., p. 216.

91. Ibid.

92. Gonzalez, pp. 66–69; Clark S. Knowlton, "Patron-Peon Patterns Among the Spanish Americans of New Mexico," *Social Forces* 41 (October 1962), pp. 13–17.

93. Gonzalez, pp. 99–100.

94. Manual Mejida, Mexico City *Excelsior*, 23 December 1967, quoted in Swadesh, p. 56.

95. Mario Gill, *Nuestros Buenos Vecinos* (Mexico: Editorial Azteca, 1964), p. 87, quoted in Blawis, p. 37.

96. Tijerina's interview with Gardner, Nabokov Papers.

97. Tijerina quoted in Los Angeles *Free Press*, 10–17 November 1967.

98. New Mexico District Attorney Alfonso Sanchez, quoted in Gardner, p. 89; Gonzalez, p. 181; and Knowlton, "The Neglected Chapters in Mexican-American History," p. 50.

99. Knowlton, "Tijerina, Hero of the Militants"; Gonzalez, p. 179.

100. Gilberto Lopez y Rivas, *The Chicanos: Life and Struggles of the Mexican Minority in the United States*, trans. and ed. Elizabeth Martinez and Gilberto Lopez y Rivas (New York: Monthly Review Press, 1974), p. 13.

101. For an extended discussion of the history-making power of fitting responses to rhetorical situations, see Lloyd F. Bitzer, "The Rhetorical Situation," *Philosophy and Rhetoric* 1 (1968), pp. 1–14; and Michael C. McGee, "In Search of 'The People': A Rhetorical Alternative," *Quarterly Journal of Speech* 61 (1975), pp. 235–249.

3

Teaching the "Truth": The Righteous Rhetoric of Cesar Chavez

In the early spring of 1962, thirty-five-year-old Cesar Chavez moved from San Jose to Delano, California, to begin organizing farm laborers into an effective union, a task most labor leaders considered impossible.[1] California farmworkers typically had been illiterate, indigent, and migratory, and growers had easily broken all farmworkers' unions since 1903.[2] Further diminishing Chavez's chances of success, he initially lacked co-workers, personal wealth, political power, or formal education past the seventh grade. The son of migrants and a former crop-picker, he appeared to be no match for the wealth and power of California agribusiness.[3]

As most successful reformers in American history have done, Chavez relied on his public communication to change the established order. During his first eleven months in Delano the 5'7", 150–pound laborer worked in the fields all day and then drove to farmworkers' camps and homes almost nightly, attending "hundreds of house meetings" while canvassing for members in eighty-seven communities within about a 100–mile radius.[4] Luis Valdez, founder of El Teatro Campesino, remembered that Chavez entered Delano as neither the "traditional bombastic Mexican revolutionary; nor was he a *gavacho*, a gringo, a white social worker type," the two types who previously had tried and failed to organize the Mexican-Americans and Filipinos who comprised the majority of farm laborers in the area.[5] "Here was Cesar," Valdez explained, "burning with a patient fire, poor like us, dark like us, talking quietly, moving people to talk about their problems, attacking the little problems first, and suggesting, always suggesting . . . solutions that seemed attainable. We didn't know it until we met him, but he was the leader we had been waiting for."[6]

Chavez's talking led to tangible accomplishments. By 1965 he had established a union with more than 2,000 dues-paying families.[7] His United Farm Workers (UFW) soon offered precedent-setting services ranging from a newspaper and credit union to health clinics and old-age benefits, and by 1972 UFW membership passed 30,000 and had affiliated with the powerful AFL-CIO.[8] UFW victories included strict agreements regarding the growers' use of pesticides which endangered workers; contracts with "most major wineries, the lettuce-growing subsidiary of United Brands, and the citrus-growing subsidiary of Coca Cola"[9] and the nation's first collective-bargaining legislation for farmworkers. Chavez's crusade, featuring strikes, marches, fasts, and speeches, established his reputation as a charismatic leader and won for the UFW statements of support ranging from the mayor and city council of San Francisco to the 1972 Democratic national platform.[10] Although the UFW temporarily lost contracts when the powerful Teamsters Union challenged it in a bitter battle to represent farmworkers, a settlement with the Teamsters in 1977 established the UFW as the sole bargaining organization for crop-pickers in California.[11]

As Chavez attracted national attention, he gained a reputation as "the most persuasive union leader to come along in a generation."[12] Although he expanded his audience to the entire nation, he maintained the dogged persistence in speaking that had typified his earlier canvassing for farm laborers. Nearly exhausted during a speaking tour in 1965, he addressed a college audience from which he was pelted by eggs and tomatoes. The weary Chavez scarcely noticed the flying food and continued calmly presenting his case—and the audience applauded him for his apparent coolness.[13] On a three-month tour in 1969 of some ninety cities in the United States and Canada, he reported that "everywhere I spoke I asked people to get hold of their

Congressmen and make a complaint. And you know, it worked."[14] In 1972 a co-worker complained that Chavez loved to organize workers, "but he can't do it because right now he has to go around speaking."[15] Listeners to the slender but energetic Chavez, a man with "an Indian's bow nose and lank black hair, with sad eyes and an open smile," included congressional committees, college students, political gatherings, Christian organizations, viewers of the national news media, and even Pope Paul VI.[16] Among those early moved by Chavez's persuasion was Dolores Huerta, who later became a leader in the UFW. After initially perceiving him as quiet and shy, she "heard him speak one time at a board meeting and . . . was really impressed."[17]

Chavez served as a major Chicano leader as well as a union leader. From its beginnings the UFW was closely identified "with the civil rights movement and its techniques of aggressive non-violence."[18] Consisting mainly of Mexican-Americans, his farm labor movement played a major role in creating the Chicano protest.[19] Although Chavez frequently emphasized union interests over ethnic issues, he became the most prominent, most revered, and only nationally recognized leader of Mexican-Americans.[20] Chicano poet Octavio Romano V gave Chavez credit for teaching the lesson that "the Mexican-American must state his case before the entire nation and stir its conscience."[21] The non-violent activist became a folk hero for many Americans of all colors and the "spiritual leader for Chicanos" during the turbulent 1960s. A wide variety of Americans shared the opinion of him expressed in *Look* magazine: "At a time when many American radicals are saying that nonviolence—as an instrument for social change—died with Martin Luther King, it is reassuring to meet a man of faith who preaches compassion rather than bloody confrontation, practices what he preaches, and gets results."[22] On ABC television's "Good Night America," host Geraldo Rivera described Chavez as "one of those really rare people, who qualifies under the heading of legend in their own time."[23] This legend grew from speeches like the one he delivered at the federal prison at McNeil Island, after which the president of the Chicano prisoners group exclaimed: "This man has brought us this dream. He has given us reason to say: 'I'm an American of

Mexican descent, and I am proud of it.' "[24] A perplexed Teamster president Jimmy Hoffa expressed a less flattering view of the idealistic Chavez: "Sure I like the guy. But he's some sort of religious fanatic in search of martyrdom. You can't run a union that way."[25]

Chavez's reliance on discourse and his ability to appeal to a broad audience, to reach "the campesino and college student alike,"[26] characterized his rhetorical campaign. Why was he so persistent in presenting his persuasive message, particularly during the early years when he faced such long odds against its success? How did he win over Mexican-Americans and Anglos alike, to become the Chicano with the broadest and largest audience? What techniques and strategies characterized his public persuasion? Why did he select these means? The key to answering these questions and thus to understanding Chavez's role as a spokesman for the Chicano movement, lies in the relationship between his theory and practice of reform rhetoric.

CHAVEZ'S VIEW OF PUBLIC DISCOURSE

The roots of Chavez's view of public discourse have been in his perceptions of God and reform and in his experience as a labor organizer. A devout Roman Catholic, he described the worldwide ecumenical church as "one form of the Presence of God on Earth" and a "powerful moral and spiritual force" in the world.[27] He has accepted orthodox Catholic positions; for example, the Church must care for the poor, and Christ's model of non-violence is admirable.[28]

In 1952 Chavez found concrete goals for his Christian convictions when he met Father Donald McDonnell, a priest who ministered to *braceros* and migrant workers and convinced Chavez to devote himself to fighting for social and legal justice for the poor and particularly for farmworkers. After discovering that churchmen did not understand how to organize underprivileged people into effective pressure groups, Chavez joined the Community Service Organization (CSO). Operating on the assumption that American institutions would respond to pressure, the CSO concentrated on organizing poor and working-class Mexican-Americans to obtain their rights.[29] In his ten years with the

CSO he learned that organizing leads to power. He also learned that organizers should expect no appreciation for their work.[30] The compensation for Chavez was in doing the will of God at the service of fellow Mexican-Americans.

As a CSO labor organizer, Chavez gained experience in public discourse and confidence in its power. He recalled that initially he was "very awkward and nervous about speaking to groups."[31] Soon, however, he began speaking frequently at various homes, often lying awake at night after the meeting, "going over the whole thing, playing the tape back, trying to see why people laugh at one point, or why they were for one thing or against another."[32] He perceived public address as necessary to organize workers, claiming that "there are some very simple things that have to be done, certain key things that nobody can do without, like talking to people."[33] "Just keep talking to people," he concluded, "and they will respond."[34] As a CSO speaker, he also learned that clear illustrations and examples were more effective in communicating ideas than was philosophizing. To reach listeners, he discovered, "you have to draw a simple picture and color it in."[35]

As a union organizer, Chavez developed a millennial interpretation of contemporary history based on his beliefs in God, the injustice suffered by the poor, the need to organize workers, and the power of public address. As the 1960s ended, he declared: "People are not going to turn back now. The poor are on the march: black, brown, red, everyone, whites included. We are now in the midst of the biggest revolution this country has ever known."[36] With the UFW consisting primarily of disadvantaged members of racial minorities, Chavez viewed union issues as civil rights issues which pitted the strong and rich against the poor and weak.[37] Therefore the UFW, he instructed, was "not just another union," but a movement "to change the conditions of human life."[38] To Chavez, then, the UFW was "a family bound together in a common struggle for justice."[39] His convictions that "our cause is just, that history is a story of social revolution, and that the poor shall inherit the land," led him to announce with assurance: "We will win, we *are* winning, because ours is a revolution of mind and heart, not only of economics."[40] Just as irreconcilable labor-management disputes can often be settled by an impartial third-party arbiter, he envisioned a human arbiter of his struggle for justice: public opinion. Convinced that "the love of justice in the hearts of other Americans is still our last and best hope," he confidently forecasted: "I contend that not only the American public but people in general throughout the world will respond to a cause that involves injustice."[41]

Chavez's view of the workings of the world undergirded his conception of rhetorical discourse. He and other farmworker-orators were crucial agents in God's plan to eliminate injustice toward the poor and minorities. To organize farmworkers and then to educate a public which would inevitably embrace a just case and accordingly right society's imperfections, these orators must present a clear message of pertinent facts and moral considerations. Despite awesome challenges and temporary setbacks, the UFW spokesman could be sure of eventual success if he persisted in presenting his case.

CHAVEZ'S PUBLIC DISCOURSE

A close examination of three addresses in which Chavez faced ethnically mixed audiences will reveal his rhetorical manner, form, and content.[42] Following this examination, connections will be made between his rhetorical means and his view of the nature and function of reform rhetoric.

On 16 May 1968, Chavez spoke for forty-eight minutes at City College of New York (CCNY).[43] He began graciously by introducing several people close to the movement and explaining that "this goes to show you that there are many, many people besides myself" in the struggle. He then turned to the broad moral theme that the farmworkers' struggle "is a very basic struggle . . . for justice" for the "poor" and "weak" against the "rich" and "powerful." The body of his speech contained two sections: he argued that unfair legislation and law enforcement built the immense wealth and power of growers while discriminating against farmworkers; and he outlined the history, needs, and protest tactics of farmworkers, including the relationship of his union to civil rights, the power of the boycott, the philosophy of civil disobedience, the advantages of non-violence, and the value of union negotiations and contracts. He finished on a high moral note. Listeners could boycott grapes to help workers who had struggled for two and one-half years "to gain that manhood that powerful forces have taken away from us." That manhood he defined simply as the right "to live, and act, and to enjoy all of the privileges as human beings."

Chavez relied heavily on statistics and examples to explain his ideas and prove his arguments. His opening argument that growers disobeyed or profited from laws is representative. He pointed out that California farmers owned farms of up to 160,000 acres, he cited a series of laws designed to aid farmers with large acreage, and he concluded by saying that California agriculture was a $5 billion industry which accounted for every third job in the state. Discussing the history of farmworkers' organizations from the turn-of-the-century Wobblies to his own union, he referred to the exact number of towns which he visited when establishing his union. He related stories of a farmworker named John who talked to Chavez until 3 A.M. one morning advocating violence, of a woman who lost her fingernails because of pesticides, and of the "many cases where a . . . farmworker has problems of vision." He mentioned the precise number of Mexican workers who daily crossed the border to work in the United States, and he employed diverse examples such as the following: the power obtained by owning land in Latin America and Asia, the anti-strike activities of the Delano Chamber of Commerce, the visit of Attorney General Ramsey Clark to California to investigate lack of enforcement of laws, and his own early conversion to non-violence. An example of the need to train military men to kill demonstrated that most men were fundamentally non-violent, and the example of Martin Luther King, Jr., illustrated that non-violence required a total commitment. To show that farmworkers needed a written contract with growers, he spun out a detailed, folksy anecdote about a deceased farmworker, Juan Garcia. Denied passage through heaven's pearly gates because he had no horse, Juan left to seek a horse and met his recently deceased employer who also lacked a horse. The employer proposed that both men could enter heaven if he rode on Juan's back, but upon reaching the gates the employer was directed to tie his "horse" outside and enter. "And this is what happened to us," Chavez pointed out; "We've been kept out of society too long" and need to bargain collectively for guaranteed rights.

Numerous signpost or transition sentences led listeners through the speech. Chavez declared early: "But I'd like to tell you a little about the power that the growers have in the West and in California in particular"; and less than a minute later he partitioned the next section of his speech: "In my opinion there are three things that make them very powerful"—land, water, and cheap farm-labor. His story of Juan Garcia began in this manner: "I remember a long time ago, talking with a farmworker . . . and he told me a story, and I'd like to tell it to you." The topics of the power of the boycott, of the relationship of his union to civil rights, and of organizing began with these respective introductions: "You may often wonder and may ask, 'Why is it that you have to boycott to win your strike?' "; "I've been asked many times, 'What are you really, a union or a civil rights movement?' and I say, 'both' "; and, "if you were to ask me which are the most important, the three most important items in the drive to organize workers, it would be very easy. I would say . . . " He introduced his examples of union organizing with, "I'd like to tell you very briefly some of the things we did."

Chavez also bridged and ended main points with clear transitions. Moving from fasting to civil rights, he said: "And then every time you speak of nonviolence and fasting, you think of civil disobedience. And I'm asked many times 'what are your views of civil disobedience?' " Or again: "Not only were the employers then passing legislation to get land, and passing legislation to get water, paid for by you, and also passing legislation on immigration, they were concerned about another area." His anecdote about Garcia finished with a clear statement of its lesson, and his arguments against the illegal entry of Mexican workers ended with: "This is the reason why we haven't won the strike."

Chavez's style was also designed for clarity. Describing how growers imported people of various nationalities to work in the fields, he disclosed that "the growers went to Japan. They went to Congress. They enacted special legislation. They brought in the Japanese." His simple language and syntax, his personal and folksy tone, stand out in one of his concluding appeals: "I'd like very much to see, and we need your help in this, no grapes—in New York City. Just, to be sure, not to make any errors, no grapes. Don't eat grapes. Don't let your friends eat grapes. Don't let the University see any grapes, in any kitchen. Just, no grapes. And, if you do that for us, we'll promise you that we'll win the strike."

Chavez's reliance on clearly organized and simply stated explanations and arguments backed by abundant facts and homey examples fits a rhetorical model appropriate for illustrating a case that had enough moral truths to speak persuasively for itself. He explicitly revealed his confidence in well-reasoned discourse on several occasions during his speech. Noting that growers "use many arguments to sell people" the viewpoint of agribusiness, he systematically refuted their major arguments. He also contended: "I can prove this" point that insecticide sprays are dangerous, and then he offered six examples to prove his point. After outlining one argument in favor of the boycott, he introduced another with the words: "There is more than one reason why you should help us in this boycott." His belief in the potency of a just case did not negate the need to adjust ideas to people, however, and he admitted: "If you were a church group, I would tell you it's a struggle for social justice. And if you were a group of labor, I'd tell you it's a struggle for economic justice. And you're a group of students, so I tell you plainly, very simply, it's a struggle against the power structure."

Chavez again appeared as a reasonable teacher of truth rather than an inflammatory rabble-rouser when he spoke first in English, then in Spanish at the Montopolis Community Center in Austin, Texas, on 6 February 1971.[44] Five thousand listeners, including supporters of La Raza, strikers against the Economy Furniture Company, and "those who came to see and hear" Chavez, heard opening words that set his persuasive tone of graciousness.

Friends, sisters, honored guests, I'm extremely pleased to be here in Austin and in Texas. I've heard so much of the warm Texas hospitality, and let me tell you that I really know what you mean when you say, when you hear in California—about Texas hospitality. . . . I think that everyone that I have come in contact with in this day and a half has been extremely gracious and courteous and friendly.

Later in the speech he acknowledged generously that "there's so many good people that must be thanked"—Texas legislators, county commissioners, people who met him at the airport. Former U.S. senator from Texas Ralph Yarborough, listening in the audience, was a long-time friend of the farmworkers and "a great man." Although he predicted a Chicano would someday be elected governor of a southwestern state, he hastened to add benevolently that he intended "no offense to the present governors of the various southwestern states."

Chavez began by briefly discussing the Economy strike and then urging a boycott of Montgomery Ward until the store discontinued its line of Economy Furniture. These immediate issues ushered in a lengthy explanation of the broader issues of what, how, and why non-violent tactics succeed in a right cause. Maintaining that workers possessed an "inherent" right to join unions in order to reach "their rightful place in society," he argued that the boycott would succeed because it was an "extension of love from one human being to the other" and thereby a "powerful weapon of the poor people and people who struggle for justice." This expression of love "creates a chain reaction that has tremendous consequences for good." To demonstrate the influence of the boycott, he used detailed anecdotes to show that American children recognized his name and had heard of the farmworkers' boycott against grapes and lettuce. Chavez asserted that once Chicanos were treated as "human beings," they would obtain political power as well as union contracts. His concern for justice extended far beyond Chicanos, however, and he called for attention to needy people regardless of race.

Chavez's conclusion in English began with an emphasis on moral questions: "The thing that all of us want—and here we're concerned for one another—is to build and not destroy. . . . And really be concerned, really for the dignity of men" in order to "change things so we can get justice and dignity for our people." Non-violence was essential, he added, to effect these changes. His conclusion in Spanish, eight paragraphs in which he urged

Chicanos to help each other and to stress education of the young, contained little except the word pictures of anecdotes and illustrations. After a lengthy Mexican anecdote ended with one cowboy telling another that he would not cut off the head of a bee because a bee is "very organized; if I harm it, I'll have thousands of its kind on me soon," he made his point: "That is how we ought to think: a wrong against any one of us is a wrong against all." Other folksy examples told of red ants organizing into a bunch, of workers in cars picking up migrants along the California roads many years ago, of a Mexican-American woman caring more for the purchase of a television set than for her mother, of Chavez's wife wanting a 1971 model car because his godmother had one, and of his twelve-year-old son supporting his lettuce boycott. Each of these examples ended or began with a statement of the appropriate lesson. The speech concluded with a lengthy Mexican story in which a government official inspecting a school in a remote and backward Mexican village asked this question to test students' knowledge of Mexican history: "Who can tell me who burned Cuauhtemoc's feet?" A young boy answered, "Listen, Mr. Inspector, we are very poor but we are very honest. I guarantee you none of us burned Cuauhtemoc's feet." Chavez then related the anecdote to the goal of education: "We must know everything, we must know who burned Cuauhtemoc's feet."

To direct listeners from topic to topic during his address, he employed these transitions: "And I'm asking you to do a couple of things"; "I'd like to tell you two short stories"; "I want to tell you one more thing"; "Let me relate a Mexican anecdote about two men"; and, "Friends, let me close by just saying . . ." In his clear and personal style he frequently referred to strikers and to himself, using "I" or "we" 108 times. For example, he recounted: "I visited with Lencho and Pancho and Cowboy and the other leaders of the strike. I visited with them. I went to the picket line. I went to their office. I went to the picket shack and I went to their homes. And, you know, it reminds me so much of Delano. So much."

Although frequently referring to himself, Chavez deemphasized his role in farmworkers' triumphs. Those victories, he argued, resulted from the drive for justice which was powered by love and its influence through the boycott. "Once you get the ideas of a boycott in motion, in track, and it begins to function on its own," he concluded, "nothing on this good earth will stop it—except a signed contract." This spirit of strikers could also effect change, and listeners were hearing not Chavez but "the spirit of our people speaking loudly today." Again he appeared humble, gracious, and thoughtful, a conduit for the powerful case for righteous reform.

On 26 September 1972, Chavez delivered a twenty-one minute speech at the University of Santa Clara, its campus troubled by student protests over the dismissal of seven minority members of the student-services staff.[45] After briefly examining the student protest and the aims and means of the worldwide movement for reform, he concentrated on the struggle between growers and farmworkers as it related to Proposition 22 on the 22 June ballot in California. He reviewed growers' efforts to prevent farmworkers from forming a union, and he recounted how farmworkers retaliated with boycotts and strikes. In his conclusion he argued that non-violence was moral, legal, and infused with "truth and tremendous power that cannot be generated in any other way."

For several minutes Chavez explicated his philosophy of the inevitability of just reform and the desirability of public discussion. Relating his topic to his particular audience, he began by declaring that the problem at Santa Clara "is pretty much like the problems out in the fields." Just as growers must talk with strikers and submit differences to an arbiter, so the university and students must discuss and negotiate before a third party. "The time has come," he explained, "when powerless and small groups of people, minority people . . . cannot be set aside or pushed aside without explanation." "These days are not days for one to make decisions based" on power alone, he claimed; "more and more throughout the world" decisions which hold up are being based on "justice" and "reason." "However lowly the man or woman making a grievance," he repeated, there must be discussion and negotiation: "after all, they all, they all are of the same human race."

Chavez's discussion of Proposition 22 bulged with facts. He pointed out that the proposition was placed on the ballot only after growers unsuccessfully proposed legislation three times in three years to stop farmworkers from organizing. The proposition's insidious provision for a sixty-day injunction against strikers would effectively end the power of strikes, because "98 percent" of "108" crops in California could be harvested in less than sixty days. Numerous other statistics and examples illustrated the potential effect of 22, the number of voters eligible to vote for farmworkers' boycotts, and the means by which a public relations firm put 22 on the ballot. Underscoring his faith in facts in a just cause, he announced that his investigation of every California county's petition to place 22 on the ballot had uncovered evidence of forgery and fraud—and he had given the evidence to the Secretary of State.

He again provided numerous signpost sentences to ensure a clear reception of his explanations and facts. He opened by forecasting his examination of the protests at Santa Clara: "We're pleased to be here this afternoon to spend a few minutes with you—to talk about the farmworker. . . . Before I do that, before I came here I met with the Chicano brothers and sisters, and they were airing a complaint to me against the administration." His discussion of 22 began with the warning, "And to this, this is what I want to talk to you about." He partitioned his following analysis in this manner: growers wanted "legislation that will do two things, that will take away our right to strike and our right to boycott"; and, 22 serves growers' needs "by very simply doing the following . . . " He introduced several examples with, "Let me give you an example in the Coachella Valley"; and "let me give you some examples" of fraudulent petitioning for 22. His discussion of laws on strikes and boycotts began with, "And it is to this that I want to speak very clearly." Reaching three sub-topics, he pointed out: "And so Proposition 22 has three hurdles to go through." Using simply phrased questions to serve as transitions, he asked: "Do you know how arrests came about? It's very simple"; and, "And the clincher is, why 60 days for an injunction? Why not 80 days? Why not 45 days? And the answer is very simple."

Chavez's persona conformed to his previous pattern. When discussing complaints by students at Santa Clara, he modestly admitted: "I want to assure you that I do not know the complaints in detail." Opponents received gracious treatment when his explanation that growers could send to jail any farmworker who tells a friend to boycott lettuce ended with these words: "I doubt that they would go that far, but that's what the law says." Continuing his faith in well-reasoned arguments, he attributed the setbacks of growers in their conflicts with workers to the problems growers had in "justifying what they are saying."

Throughout Chavez's rhetorical career his oral delivery—his use of voice and body—reinforced his persona as a gentle advocate who emphasized content over personality. Biographers reported that his speeches were "soft, sweetened by a Spanish accent" and that "what is striking in his gentle voice is his lack of mannerisms."[46] The London *Times* noted that he "overwhelmed the listener with his gentleness."[47] Protestant Minister Winthrop Yinger, who heard Chavez speak "three or four dozen times" between 1965 and 1976, described his "conversational tone of delivery. He does not punctuate his ideas with shouts; indeed, he seldom raises his voice at all."[48] Speaking slowly and deliberately, calmly and gently, Chavez appeared to trust the persuasive power of his arguments and explanations.[49]

Chavez's non-verbal communication extended past his delivery. In a well-publicized protest march in 1966 from Delano to the state capitol in Sacramento, for example, farmworkers walked under the banner of the Virgin of Guadalupe as well as the flags of Mexico and of the farmworkers.[50] In the view of Meier and Rivera, the symbolic appeal of the Virgin of Guadalupe attracted Mexican-Americans to Chavez's organization.[51] Chavez himself understood the appeal of the symbol. He explained that the basilica of the Virgin of Guadalupe was the major shrine in Mexico for pilgrims, many of whom walked on their knees during the final mile or two. "Made with sacrifice and hardship as an expression of penance and of commitment," this trip often included a request to the patron for benefits "of body or soul."[52] Thus, the Mexicans' religious pilgrimage paralleled that of protesting farmworkers who also offered their suffering and commitment to a moral cause in which they expected success.

SUMMARY AND CONCLUSIONS

Chavez's discourse, as illustrated by his speeches at CCNY, Austin, and Santa Clara, contained distinctive features. He employed lucid explanations and arguments, illustrated with plentiful facts, simple anecdotes, and concrete examples. He added clarity to his case through abundant transitions and a simple style. Elevating his message and himself above purely practical, pragmatic, or selfish interests, he stressed moral issues and treated opponents generously. His case for supporting his union fit into his broader argument that racial minorities, in particular Mexican-Americans, were being swept ineluctably by Providence toward the economic, social, and political justice they deserved. His calm delivery further focused attention on his message rather than on himself. Not neglecting rhetorical concerns, he adapted his topics to immediate audiences and pressing issues. These same characteristics emerged in numerous other speeches and formed his rhetorical profile.[53]

Chavez's discourse persuaded Anglos as well as Mexican-Americans. For Chicanos, he employed conventionally powerful patterns, forms, and appeals: folksaying and *dichos* or maxims; anecdotes and stories or *cuentos*; Spanish formality, graciousness, and respect, as illustrated by his warm and respectful acknowledgments in introductions; and familial and religious themes and images, which surfaced in his references to God and his examples of and quotes about Mexican, Mexican-American, and southwestern families.[54] On occasion his allegiance with the Virgin of Guadalupe further linked his cause and calls to action with the religion and culture of Mexican-Americans. To Anglo idealists in the idealistic 1960s, moreover, he was also an ideal spokesman—one with a case built on abundant facts and high moral principles. That case, because it was presented so calmly and clearly, appeared to trust the good judgment of right-minded listeners regardless of color.

Chavez's rhetorical posture as a calm teacher of truth may be unusual for an ethnic activist or militant labor organizer, but it is not surprising in light of his conception of rhetorical discourse. Influenced by his experiences as a labor organizer and by his views of religion and reform, he saw himself as playing a crucial role in God's plan to right injustices suffered by the poor. The temporal means to these divine ends was the American public which, when well informed, would effectuate appropriate reforms. His job was not primarily to inspire militant action on a particular issue but to educate audiences about farmworkers' moral struggles and tactics. Hence, he relied on facts and clarity, focusing on the power of his ideas rather than on his personal accomplishments, and he avoided vilifying opponents or haranguing audiences, preferring to let his explanations and arguments speak for themselves. Influencing the quantity as well as the quality of his public address, his faith in the ultimate success of his morally right rhetoric motivated him to present his case persistently despite awesome obstacles to success. In the end, Chavez's victories may have justified his faith in righteous rhetoric.

NOTES

1. Matt S. Meier and Feliciano Rivera, *The Chicanos: A History of Mexican-Americans* (New York: Hill and Wang, 1972), p. 258; Peter Matthiessen, *Sal Si Puedes: Cesar Chavez and the New American Revolution* (New York: Random House, 1969), p. 4.

2. Matthiessen, pp. 4–5.

3. Joan London and Henry Anderson, *So Shall Ye Reap* (New York: Thomas Y. Crowell, 1970), p. 147; Meier and Rivera, p. 261. A migrant worker from the age of ten, Chavez attended over thirty schools but never reached high school. Matthiessen, p. 227. There are a number of books on Chavez and his farmworkers' movement. The most detailed are the first-hand accounts of Jacques Levy, *Cesar Chavez: Autobiography of La Causa* (New York: W. W. Norton and Co., 1975); Peter Matthiessen, *Sal Si Puedes*; and Mark Day, *Forty Acres: Cesar Chavez and the Farm Workers* (New York: Praeger, 1971). Especially valuable for background on the farm labor movement and its key supporters are London and Anderson; Eugene Nelson, *Huelga: The First Hundred Days of the Great Delano Grape Strike* (Delano: Farm Workers Press, 1966); and Ronald B. Taylor, *Chavez and the Farm Workers* (Boston: Beacon Press, 1975). Other helpful books on Chavez and the farmworkers are: Steve Allen, *The Ground Is Our Table* (New York: Doubleday and Co., 1966); John Gregory Dunne, *Delano* (New York: Farrar, Straus and Giroux, 1971); Ernesto Galarza, *Spiders in the House and Workers in the Field* (Notre Dame, Ind.: University of Notre Dame Press, 1970); Dick Meister and Anne Loftis, *A Long Time Coming: The Struggle to Unionize America's Farm Workers* (New York: Macmillan Co., 1977); Jean Maddern Pitrone, *Chavez: Man of the Migrants* (New York: Pyramid Books, 1972); and Winthrop Yinger, *Cesar Chavez: The Rhetoric of Nonviolence* (New York: Exposition Press, 1975).

4. Matthiessen, p. 6; Peter Barnes, "The Future of the United Farm Workers: Chavez Against the Wall," *The New Republic*, 7 December 1974, p. 13; Cesar Chavez, "Cesar Chavez: Grass-Roots Organizer," in *Aztecas Del Norte: The Chicanos of Aztlan*, ed. Jack D. Forbes (Greenwich, Conn.: Fawcett Publications, 1973), p. 281; Cesar Chavez, "Why Delano?", in *Aztlan: An Anthology of Mexican-American Literature*, ed. Luis Valdez and Stan Steiner (New York: Alfred A. Knopf, 1972), pp. 203–204.

5. Luis Valdez, "The Tale of La Raza," *Ramparts*, July 1966, p. 40.

6. Valdez, p. 40.

7. "Membership Grows: New Benefits and Services," *El Malcriado*, No. 26, 22 December 1965.

8. Taylor, pp. 219 and 13–14. Chavez's organization has had several names, including the United Farm Workers Organizing Committee (UFWOC). In this study we will refer to his organization as the UFW.

9. Barnes, p. 14. UFW's side of the farmworker-grower conflict is reported in *El Malcriado*, the UFW newspaper, Keene, California. The growers' point-of-view is in *California Farm Bureau Monthly*.

10. A wide variety of observers have labeled Chavez charismatic. See, for examples, *Fourteenth Report of the Senate Factfinding Committee on Un-American Activities* (Senate of the State of California, 1967), p. 19; "The Communists," cited in Gary Allen, "The Grapes: Communist Wrath in Delano," pamphlet (Belmont, Mass.: American Opinion, 1966), p. 3; Clark S. Knowlton, "The Neglected Chapters in Mexican-American History," in *Mexican-Americans Tomorrow*, ed. Gus Tyler (Albuquerque: University of New Mexico Press, 1967), p. 46.

11. Tom Nicholson and William J. Cook, "Cesar's Triumph," *Newsweek*, 21 March 1977, pp. 70 and 72.

12. Charles Kuralt, narrator, "The State of the Union," CBS television documentary, Summer 1966. A partial transcript of this document is in the San Joaquin Valley Farm Workers Collection, Special Collections Department, Library, Fresno State University.

13. Matthiessen, p. 112.

14. "A Continuing Conversation with Cesar Chavez," *Journal of Current Social Issues* 9 (Spring 1971), p. 31.

15. Dolores Huerta, "Dolores Huerta Talks About Republicans, Cesar, Children, and Her Home Town," *La Voz del Pueblo* (November-December 1972), rpt. in *An Awakening Minority: The Mexican Americans*, ed. Manual P. Serven, 2d ed. (Beverly Hills: Glencoe Press, 1970), p. 289.

16. Chavez's speeches on varied occasions are described in *El Malcriado*. See also note 53; Chavez's audience with the Pope is cited in Levy, pp. 524–525.

17. Huerta, p. 286.

18. Barnes, p. 14.

19. Tony Castro, *Chicano Power: The Emergence of Mexican America* (New York: Saturday Review Press, 1974), p. 13; Jack D. Forbes, "The Awakening of 1966–68," in Forbes, pp. 283–284. In its widely publicized Plan of Delano in 1966, the UFW proclaimed itself to be "sons of the Mexican Revolutionary, a revolution of the poor seeking bread and justice." The Plan is in Valdez and Steiner, pp. 197–99 and in *El Malcriado*, No. 31, 17 March 1966.

20. Ruth S. Lamb, *Mexican-Americans: Sons of the Southwest* (Claremont, Calif.: Ocelot Press, 1970), p. 2; "The Little Strike That Grew to La Causa," *Time*, 4 July 1969, p. 16; "The Chicanos Campaign for a Better Deal," *Business Week*, 29 May 1971, p. 48; Castro, p. 96.

21. "Preface," in *Voices: Readings from El Grito*, ed. Octavio I. Romano V (Berkeley: Quinto Sol Publications, 1971), p. 9.

22. Meier and Rivera, p. 258; introduction to Cesar Chavez, "Nonviolence Still Works," *Look*, 1 April 1969, p. 52.

23. "Dirt Cheap," ABC Television, 30 July 1973.

24. Quoted in Don Hannula, "Chavez Welcomed at McNeil," *Seattle Times*, 19 December 1969.

25. Quoted in "The Farmworkers' Prophet," (London) *Daily Times*, 2 September 1973.

26. Ellwyn R. Stoddard, *Mexican Americans* (New York: Random House, 1973), p. 204.

27. Cesar E. Chavez, "The Mexican-American and the Church," a paper presented at the Second Annual Mexican-American Conference in Sacramento, 8–10 March 1968, in *Voices: Readings from El Grito*, ed. Octavio Romano V, p. 101.

28. Chavez, "The Mexican-American and the Church," p. 104.

29. Levy, p. 91; Chavez interviewed by Bob Fitch, "Tilting with the System: An Interview with Cesar Chavez," *Christian Century*, 18 February 1970, pp. 206–207, Alfredo Cuellar, "Perspective on Politics," Chapter 8, in *Mexican Americans*, ed. Joan W. Moore (Englewood Cliffs, N.J.: Prentice-Hall, 1970), p. 146.

30. Chavez, "Cesar Chavez: Grass-Roots Organizer," p. 280.

31. Chavez, "Nonviolence Still Works," p. 57.

32. Cesar Chavez, "The Organizer's Tale," *Ramparts*, July 1966, pp. 44–46.

33. Chavez quoted in Levy, p. 161.

34. Chavez quoted in Matthiessen, pp. 284–85.

35. Chavez, "The Organizer's Tale," p. 44; Chavez quoted in Matthiessen, pp. 48–49.

36. Chavez quoted in Day, p. 12.

37. Chavez quoted in "Cesar Chavez Talks in New York," *Catholic Worker*, June 1968. An unpaginated copy of this article is in the San Joaquin Valley Farm Workers Collection, Fresno State University (FSU) Library.

38. Chavez quoted in "El Malcriado: The Voice of the Farm Worker," in Valdez and Steiner, p. 208.

39. *Statement by Cesar Chavez on the Conclusion of a 25 Day Fast for Non-Violence*, Delano, 10 March 1968. The Reverend James Drake read this statement for the weakened Chavez. The text minus its introduction is in Valdez and Steiner, pp. 386–387. The full text, in mimeograph form, is in the San Joaquin Valley Farm Workers Collection, FSU Library.

40. Cesar Chavez to E. L. Barr, Delano, Good Friday, 1969, in *Pain and Promise: The Chicano Today*, ed. Edward Simmen (New York: Mentor Books, 1972), p. 31; interview with Chavez, "Nonviolence Still Works," p. 57.

41. Chavez, "Nonviolence Still Works," p. 56; Chavez, "Tilting with the System: An Interview with Cesar Chavez," p. 204.

42. Our entire sample of Chavez's discourse as well as another critic's observations about his speaking manner are cited in note 53. Other speeches by Chavez are housed in the Labor History Archives at Wayne State University but were unavailable to scholars.

43. An audiotape of this speech is in the Latin American Library of the Oakland Public Library, Oakland, California.

44. A description of Chavez's audience and a twenty-two page transcript of this speech are in the appendix to Robert Tice, "The Rhetoric of La Raza," unpublished manuscript, 1971. This book-length manuscript is housed in the Chicano Studies Collection, Hayden Library, Arizona State University, Tempe.

45. An audiotape of this speech was obtained from Professor Matt S. Meier, Department of History, Santa Clara University, Santa Clara, California.

46. Levy, p. xv; Matthiessen, p. 173.

47. "The Farmworkers' Prophet," p. 63.

48. Yinger, pp. 21 and 48. This book grew out of Yinger's master's degree thesis (Fresno State University) and concentrates on Chavez's speech at the conclusion of his twenty-five day fast, 10 March 1968.

49. These qualities in Chavez's delivery emerge clearly in the taped and live speeches cited in note 53.

50. Rodolfo Acuña, *Occupied America: The Chicano's Struggle Toward Liberation* (San Francisco: Canfield Press, 1972), pp. 224 and 179; Meier and Rivera, pp. 265–266.

51. Meier and Rivera, p. 263.

52. Cesar Chavez, "Peregrination, Penitencia, Revolucion," in Valdez and Steiner, p. 385.

53. This rhetorical profile characterized seven other complete speeches of Chavez studied by the authors. The seven are: Chavez's speech at the conclusion of his twenty-five day fast in Delano, 10 March 1968; "A Transcript of a Hearing with Cesar Chavez," U.S. House of Representatives Education and Labor Committee, 1 October 1969, 33 pp.; "Statement of Cesar E. Chavez" to the Subcommittee on Labor of the U.S. Senate Committee on Labor and Public Welfare, 16 April 1969, 14 pp.; Chavez's speech at "Religious Leaders Conference," Delano, 5 June 1970 (audiotape provided by Chaplin Winthrop Yinger, California Maritime Academy, Vallejo, California); "Cesar Chavez on Money and Organizing," speech delivered to a church group, Keene, California, 4 October 1971, 7 pp. (text available at San Joaquin Valley Farm Workers Collection FSU Library); Chavez's speech at Chabot College, Hayward, California, 2 May 1975; and Chavez's speech at San Jose City College, 6 October 1976 (audiotape available at the San Jose City College Library). Yinger noted many of these same rhetorical characteristics. He found that Chavez did not "employ flamboyant and fiery oratory" (p. 47); that "economy of words, structure and style are common in all his speaking" (p. 48); that he used a "personalized tone" with many personal pronouns (pp. 48–49); and that he "rarely, if ever, publicly castigates individuals"—despite personal attacks on him from members of the John Birch Society and spokesmen for growers (pp. 52 and 68–71). A concern with non-violence surfaces in "*all* the rhetoric of Chavez and in most of his life style" (p. 59), Yinger added.

54. Numerous authors have cited the extensive and characteristic use of these patterns, forms, and appeals in Mexican-American discourse. For examples of such discussions, see John C. Hammerback, "An Interview with Bert Corona," *Western Journal of Speech Communication* 44 (Summer 1980), pp. 215, 218–219; Joseph E. Samora, Jr., "Rhetorica al Estilo Chicano: Some Basic Concepts from a Chicano's Viewpoint," paper presented at the Western Speech Communication Association Convention, Phoenix, November 1977; John Condon, " . . . So Near the United States: Notes on Communication Between Mexicans and North Americans," *The Bridge* 5 (Spring 1980), pp. 2–4, 30.

4

"No Revolutions Without Poets": The Rhetoric of Rodolfo "Corky" Gonzales

Rodolfo "Corky" Gonzales of Denver emerged as one of the most militant leaders in the Chicano movement. Although each Chicano leader could be described as militant, Gonzales has stood out because

his militancy is of a very special nature. It is an unusual combination of compassion and anger; idealism and stern realism. His love for La Raza is demonstrated every time he speaks. . . . He is angered by the Anglo's rape of our Chicano culture and his iconoclastic attacks on the Anglo hit the very conscience of the American majority.[1]

Gonzales's blend of compassion and anger, idealism and realism, was too intense and emotional to be confined to public speaking. His most influential statement took another form of communication: poetry. An integral part of the workings of the early Chicano movement rather than a mere romantic appendage to it, poetry was read or performed for crowds at political rallies and published in movement newspapers in order to inspire and inform. Rudolph O. de la Garza and Rowena Rivera describe its significance: "These early writings [during the 1960s], most of which are poetry, are closely related to the rise of Chicano militancy. They served to feed the movement and were the medium through which Chicanos became politically aware and active."[2] Gonzales himself received widespread attention from his poem *Yo Soy Joaquin* (I Am Joaquin); yet this poem was only part of his extensive rhetorical campaign.[3] Because many of his themes grew out of his personal experiences, this chapter will begin with an examination of his early life.

GONZALES'S BACKGROUND

Rodolfo "Corky" Gonzales was born in Denver, Colorado, on 18 June 1928, the son of a migrant agricultural worker. Although the family lived in Denver, each spring and summer Gonzales worked in the sugar-beet fields with his father.[4] During the fall and winter his family returned to Denver, and Gonzales attended public school. "Yes, I am a city man," he explained, "but I did a lot of farm work. I have relatives in the villages in the San Luis Valley. Every spring and summer, as a boy, I worked in the fields. Every fall and winter I lived in the city slums."[5] His experiences in the city and as a field laborer enabled Gonzales to understand and appreciate both urban and rural life. Because of his family's itinerant life, young Rodolfo attended four grade schools, three junior high schools, and two high schools. At these schools, he recalled, teachers taught him "how to forget Spanish, to forget my heritage, to forget who I am."[6] When he graduated at the age of sixteen, he had developed a lifelong hatred for the Anglo educational institution which first came into collision with his heritage.

After high school Gonzales worked in a slaughterhouse and turned to boxing: "I became a fighter because it was the fastest way to get out of the slaughterhouse. So I thought."[7] He had sufficient talent to become a National Amateur Champion and as a professional was ranked in the top ten in the featherweight division. In his poetry Gonzales described his career in the ring:

> I bleed as the vicious gloves of hunger
>   cut my face and eyes,
> as I fight my way from stinking barrios
>   to the glamour of the ring
>   and lights of fame
>   or mutilated sorrow.[8]

In 1955 Gonzales retired from boxing. Following employment as a packing-house worker, lumberjack, and farmworker, he opened a gym for barrio youth and became an after-dinner speaker on inspirational themes. "Like all boys growing up in this society," he remembered, "I identified success by wanting to be an important person loved by everyone."[9]

Gonzales's fame as a boxer opened doors to him in politics and business. In 1957 he became the first Mexican-American to attain the rank of district captain in the Denver Democratic party, and in 1960 he headed the Viva Kennedy campaign in Colorado.[10] He bought a bail-bond business and soon added an automobile agency to his holdings. By 1963 he had been promoted to general agent for the Summit Fidelity and Surety Company of Colorado.[11]

Gonzales remained active in Democratic politics. In 1963 he organized Los Voluntarios, "a political activist unit which sought more political representation for the Mexican-American community in Denver."[12] His activities resulted in his being named director of the Neighborhood Youth Corps in Denver and chairman of the board of the War on Poverty Program in Denver. By 1965 he was frequently mentioned as a future federal or state officeholder.[13] But at this time he resigned his post and abandoned his promising career in politics. He concluded: "I was used by the Democratic Party. I was used because I had a rapport with my people. Working in the two-party system I found out one thing . . . My people were exploited and men like I was are."[14]

In 1965 Gonzales founded the Crusade for Justice as an alternative to Establishment politics. Meier and Rivera isolated the reason for its founding:

He established the Crusade as a vehicle by which the objectives and priorities of the Chicano movement could be articulated and carried out. Basically a civil-rights organization, its demands . . . include reformation of the police and courts, better housing, relevant education for Chicanos, greater and more diverse employment opportunities, and land reform.[15]

Designed to meet the day-to-day needs of its members, the Crusade provides educational, legal, medical, and financial services for Chicanos in the Denver barrio.[16]

By 1968 Gonzales had developed much of his vision for the future of Chicanos. At the Poor People's March on Washington he issued his "Plan of the Barrio" which called "for housing that would meet Chicano cultural needs; for education, basically in the Spanish language; for Chicano-owned businesses to be developed in the barrio of Denver . . . and for reforms in landholding, with emphasis on the restitution of pueblo lands owned and developed by the Gringo."[17] This proclamation demonstrated Gonzales's faith in the use of rhetorical statements that were intended for mass audiences. The issuing of such statements became a standard part of his rhetorical campaign.

Gonzales and the Crusade for Justice in 1969 hosted the first national Chicano Youth Conference. Gonzales disclosed the purpose of the conference:

I thought about all the young people who are confused and who don't want to identify with these old *politicos*, those old figureheads. They don't want to identify with the same old answers. They want to get into doing something. I talked to a lot of these young people, and they decided they needed a conference. They wanted to come to Denver. So, we decided to hold it here.[18]

Christine Marin believed that

the historic significance of the Chicano Youth Liberation Conference should not be overlooked. This was the first time in the history of the Movement that a massive gathering of youths from various areas of the Southwest would agree to discuss and suggest social, educational, and political changes which would benefit the Chicanos in the rest of the United States. This was also the first time that the themes of ethnic pride, nationalism, and self-determination would be the essential elements in the unification of other Chicanos throughout the Southwest.[19]

The conference resulted in the publication of "El Plan de Aztlan," a document "which would serve as a plan or ideology to unite other Mexican Americans at various conferences in years to come," and which clearly demonstrated "the growing concept of ethnic nationalism and a self-determination among Chicanos in the entire Southwest."[20] This document, participants at the conference decided, must be "presented at every meeting, dem-

onstration, confrontation, courthouse, institution, administration, church, school, tree, building, car, and every place of human
existence."[21]

In 1970 Gonzales announced the formation of the Colorado
La Raza Unida party in which he was elected state chairman.
Two years later he became a candidate for the position of chairman of the national La Raza Unida Party, losing to Jose Angel
Gutierrez in a hotly disputed election.[22] Disagreements in that
election created a conflict which split the two leaders and re-
duced solidarity among Chicano leaders and their respective
movements.

Gonzales's background placed him in an unusually powerful
position to call for Chicano nationalism. He understood both
rural and urban Chicano life, and his fame as a boxer provided
him with excellent opportunities in Establishment businesses
and politics, something rare for a Chicano from the barrio. After
tasting and rejecting Anglo-America's "good life," he was prepared to call authoritatively and wholeheartedly for Chicano
nationalism. For him, the alternative had been sampled and
found insufficient. Moreover, as a political organizer for the
Democratic party he had attained skills necessary to build his
Chicano political organization. Too, his image as a successful
boxer projected the quality of manliness which appealed to the
Chicano's sense of machismo.

Although newsworthy for his accomplishments in business
and politics, Gonzales achieved eminence in the Chicano movement as its foremost poet. Upon publication in 1967, *Yo Soy
Joaquin* quickly became a standard reference among Chicanos.
Between 1967 and 1972 the Crusade for Justice distributed over
100,000 copies of the poem. *Yo Soy Joaquin* was reprinted in
numerous Chicano newspapers; "quoted over and over by
speakers and books dealing with the contemporary Chicano";
performed by theatre groups, young Chicanos at speech meets,
beauty contests, and dramatic readings; and cited in speeches
and essays by various Chicano leaders. All contemporary Chi-
cano-study bibliographies present it as required reading.[23] Rodolfo Acuña classified the poem as probably "the most inspiring
piece of movement literature written in the 1960s. Its impact was
immeasurable."[24] The use of poetry met the desires of early

Chicano leaders, for as "El Plan de Aztlan" directed: "We must insure that our writers, poets, musicians, and artists produce literature and art that is appealing to our people and relates to our revolutionary culture. Our cultural values of life, family, and home will serve as a powerful weapon to defeat the Gringo dollar value system and encourage the process of love and brotherhood."[25]

In the introduction to the published version of the poem, Gonzales detailed the function of his vision:

There is no inspiration without identifiable images, there is no conscience without the sharp knife of truthful exposure, and ultimately, there are no revolutions without poets.... *I Am Joaquin* became a historical essay, a social statement, a conclusion of our *mestisaje*, a welding of the oppressor (Spanish) and the oppressed (Indian). It is a mirror of our greatness and our weakness, a call to action as a total people, emerging from a glorious history, traveling through social pain and conflicts, confessing our weaknesses while we shout about our strength, culminating into one: the psychological wounds, cultural genocide, social castration, nobility, courage, determination, and the fortitude to move on to make new history for an ancient people dancing on a modern stage.[26]

The powerful animating vision of *Yo Soy Joaquin*, however, is only a part of Gonzales's broader rhetorical campaign. Through many public speeches, essays, conference "plans," and plays, he presented his message indefatigably.

THE OPPRESSED CHICANO

One of the major rhetorical problems faced by Chicano leaders in the 1960s and 1970s was the need to educate Chicanos about their treatment by Anglo institutions. Once Chicanos recognized their present situation, leaders could begin to unite them to achieve a better way of life. Without a shared vision of their common problems, and without agreement on the cause of these problems, Chicanos would remain isolated individuals or small groups with little hope of an improved life for their minority group as a whole.

Gonzales tried to raise awareness among his people by arguing that the Anglo destroyed the capacity of Chicanos to run their own lives. According to Gonzales, the destruction of the Chicano's self-image began when the Anglo first arrived in America; Anglos convinced Chicanos that nothing was "discovered" in America until "the gringo got there with a cross and a gun."[27] The Anglo's destructive treatment of Chicanos and the one remaining thread of hope—cultural identity—are described in *Yo Soy Joaquin*:

> I am Joaquin
> lost in a world of confusion
> caught up in the whirl of a
>   gringo society,
> confused by the rules,
> scorned by attitudes,
> suppressed by manipulation
> and destroyed by modern society.
> My fathers
>   have lost the economic battle
> and won
>   the struggle of cultural survival.[28]

In his rhetorical discourse, Gonzales outlined the steps used to suppress Chicano leaders. Those steps can be clustered into nine areas: (1) the Anglo power structure co-opts all potential leaders; (2) Chicanos are forced into two political parties that work against their interests; (3) Anglos control Chicanos through the educational system; (4) the legal system effectively keeps Chicanos in a subservient position; (5) the Anglo-controlled media perpetuate negative stereotypes of Chicanos; (6) Anglos divide Chicanos, causing them to fight one another; (7) Chicanos are forced off the land and into barrios where they can be controlled; (8) the leaders of the Catholic Church work against Chicanos; and (9) Anglos steal the best from Chicano culture and belittle what they reject.

Co-opting Potential Leaders

Once a leader of the Democratic party in Denver, Gonzales left his post because he felt used by the Democratic party. Extending his own example, he argued that every Mexican-American politician who held an office was "absorbed into the Anglo establishment and castrated by it."[29] The intense image of castration recurred in Gonzales's discourse. The image communicates the total and irreversible nature of co-opting and its result: the devastating loss of capacity for pleasure, manliness, and life itself. Gonzales explained how the process occurs: "Too often we have a militant leader this year; next year he has some minor job with the U.S. Government dealing with Mexican or Latin American problems, and we never hear of him again. He's become *their* Chicano."[30] Thus, Gonzales's experiences in the Democratic party taught him that Chicanos must refuse to be co-opted but continue to work for their people.

Political Parties

Chicano leaders had been exploited by political parties as well as co-opted by the Establishment. Although some Chicano leaders have abandoned the Democratic party, the traditional home of Chicanos, Gonzales saw no reason to expect better treatment by Republicans. Because each of the parties is "a monster with two heads that eats from the same trough," the Chicano always ends up as a pawn in the political game.[31] "The Republicans have given us window dressing," he explained, "while the Democrats have given the Mexican a philosophy which sounds good but never happens."[32] The Democrats gave Chicanos jobs that seemed to be important but were not. The treatment by the Democrats "does not change the social problems of different ethnic and minority groups."[33]

Gonzales dismissed the arguments among Chicanos about which party was better for them as "a bunch of garbage."[34] While the Chicanos argued, "the same Republicans and Democrats are having cocktails together at the same bar and playing golf together and kissing each other behind the scenes."[35] Therefore, Gonzales directed Chicanos to reject both political parties, because "the old methods are passé; the involvement in politics in two political bodies that are stagnant, that are status quo, have nothing to offer us."[36] Gonzales's rhetoric again reflected his past, as his political experiences convinced him that only a third party could bring political power to Chicanos: "POLITICAL LIBERATION can only come through independent action on our part, since the two-party system is the same animal with two heads that feed from the same trough. Where we are a majority, we will control; where we are a majority, we will represent a pressure group; nationally, we will represent one party: *La Familia De La Raza!*"[37]

Control of Education and the Military

Some of Gonzales's harshest criticism deals with the education—or lack of it—received by young Chicanos. He remembered that his own education was inferior and that teachers forced him to reject his language and his heritage.[38] The "hypocrisy of the U.S. educational system is without par," he reasoned, because "this education leads the Mexican to reject his own people, his home and his environment."[39] The educational system conditioned Chicano children to identify with the Anglo's image of success, an image based solely on money: "As long as he has the dollar he is a success whether he is a liar, a hypocrite or what have you."[40] Thus, young Chicanos were forced to "commit social and ethnic suicide and try to portray something they're not. They try to act and behave and think gringo."[41] Accepting the Anglo image of success, then, caused Chicanos to lose their sense of identity. As Gonzales stated in his poetry:

> And now!
>   I must choose
>   between
> the paradox of
> victory of the spirit,
> despite physical hunger,
>   or
>   to exist in the grasp
> of American social neurosis,
> sterilization of the soul
>   and a full stomach.[42]

Unfortunately, the young Mexican-American could choose only between the Anglo image of success and the Mexican-American image of defeat. The high price for choosing the positive image, Gonzales stated, was "ethnic suicide."[43]

Not only had Anglos fastened their standards of success on Chicanos, but they also reinforced the negative image of defeat in the Mexican-American community through the teaching of history in Anglo-dominated schools.

> Joaquin,
> in a country that has wiped out
> all my history,
>   stifled all my pride,
> in a country that has placed a
> different weight of indignity upon
>   my
>   age-
>   old
>   burdened back,
>   Inferiority
> is the new load.[44]

Adhering to an Anglo image of success and unaware of Chicano history, malleable Chicanos and other minorities were "told by their school teachers, probation officers to join the army. They can eat three meals, wear a new suit and be taught how to be an engineer in six months."[45] Gonzales adopted the frequently heard argument that Chicanos had done more than their share in fighting America's wars. According to him, "the only time we're afforded any of the real contributions we give this nation . . . is when we die overseas for somebody else's battle."[46] Gonzales's poetry described his view:

> My blood runs pure in the ice-caked
> hills of the Alaskan isles,
> on the corpse-strewn beach of Normandy,
> the foreign land of Korea
>   and now
>   Vietnam.[47]

In "El Plan de Aztlan" Gonzales called for an alternative educational system: "EDUCATION must be relative to our people, i.e., history, culture, bilingual education, contributions, etc. Community control of our schools, our teachers, our administrators, our counselors, and our programs."[48] As long as Anglos controlled the schools, it would be impossible to instill pride in the past accomplishments of Mexican-Americans. Pride in the Chicano heritage was necessary for a strong self-image.

Legal System and Police

Like political parties and the educational system, the legal system kept Chicanos in a second-class citizenship status. Gonzales often had violent confrontations with the police and courts, so it was not surprising that he saw them as instruments of oppression.[49] He believed that the police made "the Chicano the bad guy. They did that with the Panthers and they hope to do that with us."[50] Because the legal system supported the police attacks on Chicanos, he argued, Chicanos had little recourse: "How can there be justice," he asked, "if we don't have our people on the jury system?"[51] Chicanos—depicted as a powerless group dominated by the Establishment—could be animated to challenge and eventually control the police and legal system once made aware of their condition.

Media Stereotypes

The news media was seen as another finger on the Anglo hand that strangled Chicanos. "Newspapers do not report violence to Mexican-Americans;"[52] the media place "the Mexican American in a second-class category";[53] and reporters transform Chicanos into villains: "The man with a mustache," lectured Gonzales, "usually symbolizes the guy with a knife in his pocket. . . . He's usually the bandit . . . he's the pimp or the prostitute."[54] This stereotype by the media conditioned Chicanos to accept an inferior status, with the result that they "have been brainwashed by the media."[55] Gonzales urged Chicanos to examine their image so that they could improve it and control the view presented by the media.

Fighting Each Other

The brainwashing of Chicanos created their desire to receive social acceptance and material prosperity from the Anglo Establishment. Some Chicanos "cut their own brethren's throats to be a part of the system," lamented Gonzales.[56] Anglos developed this tactic to divide Chicanos and convince them to reject their own way of life. Thus, a successful Chicano was often defined as one who escaped the barrio and his or her past. Because such escapes were a means of dividing the Chicano community, Chicanos must become aware of this tactic. To prevent such division, Gonzales warned that Chicanos must carefully organize within their culture.

Land

Land was central to the Chicano heritage. Gonzales described the results of the Chicanos' broken ties to the land:

> My knees are caked with mud
> My hands calloused from the hoe.
> I have made the Anglo rich,
> yet
> equality is but a word—
> the Treaty of Hidalgo has been broken
> and is but another treacherous promise.
> My land is lost
> and stolen,
> My culture has been raped.
> I lengthen
> the lines at the welfare door
> and fill the jails with crime.[57]

Not only had Anglos forced Chicanos off land, but also the loss of this land had forced large numbers of people who grew up in a rural area to move to the city.[58] To some Mexican-American writers the "city is one big conspiracy to destroy the creativity of Raza and breed defeatism, to take away our sense of dignity and encourage self-hatred."[59] Chicanos moved from the land "to the unplowable concrete of the big cities."[60] The result was devastating:

The *campesino*, the men, the *caballeros* from the *ranchitos*, the migrant laborers, the villagers, the people from the mountain villages. What do they bring to the city and this society? They bring honesty. If nothing else they bring a purity that can never be matched. And what does this society and this city do to them? Why do we end up on the bottom of the ladder economically? Why do we end up on the top of the ladder in the juvenile courts and in the phony institutions? It's because we are oppressed. And this is where society destroys us.[61]

To overcome this destruction, Gonzales called for a reacquisition of land: "Land and realty ownership will be acquired by the community for the people's welfare. Economic ties of responsibility must be secured by nationalism and the Chicano defense units."[62]

The Catholic Church

Like the land, the Catholic Church was a powerful force in the lives of Chicanos. In Gonzales's view, the Church had often been a negative force because of the power of the priests. He argued that the priest will "tell you how to eat, where to go, who to sleep with and how to do it right—while he's copping everything else out. You know we're tired of this kind of leadership."[63] Such priests made Chicanos "strangers in our own church."[64]

Instead of priests who represent the dominant culture, Gonzales envisioned Church leaders who helped Chicanos:

As Christian church took its place
   in God's good name,
to take and use my virgin strength and
                  trusting faith,
the priests,
     both good and bad,
          took—
but

gave a lasting truth that
Spaniard
Indian
Mestizo
we're all God's children
And
from those words grew men
who prayed and fought
for
their own worth as human beings
for
that
GOLDEN MOMENT
of
FREEDOM.[65]

Stealing Our Culture

Anglos, Gonzales asserted, robbed what they considered positive in the Chicano culture and belittled the rest. Yet the materialistic Anglo unwittingly left intact the heart of the Chicano culture, the spirit and soul of Chicanismo, and thereby ensured the beginning of a new Chicano nationalism. As Gonzales wrote in *Yo Soy Joaquin*:

They frowned upon our way of life
and took what they could use.
Our art
Our literature,
Our music, they ignored—
so they left the real things of value
and grabbed at their own destruction
by their greed and avarice.
They overlooked that cleansing fountain of
nature and brotherhood
which is Joaquin.
The art of our great senores
Diego Rivera
Siqueiros,
Orozco, is but
another act of revolution for
the salvation of mankind,

> Mariachi music, the
>   heart and soul
>   of the people of the earth
>   the life of the child
>   and the happiness of love.[66]

When Chicanos retained their culture, instructed Gonzales, they would have a vehicle for unity: "CULTURAL values of our people strengthen our identity and the moral backbone of the movement. Our culture unites and educates the family of *La Raza* towards liberation with one heart and one mind."[67]

THE REVOLUTIONARY MOVEMENT

Once he helped the Chicano people to identify and understand their problems, Gonzales strove to create a vehicle for change. This vehicle was "a national movement of Mexican and Spanish in the Southwest . . . a militant movement that is not afraid to be linked with the spirit of Zapata, nor shy from the need to change the system, to have a social revolution."[68] Gonzales found ideological labels for the movement because "when you start to identify with the needs of the people, then you are no longer concerned with trying to define it in intellectual terms."[69]

Gonzales exhorted people to join in the revolution because "you're going to change something. . . . And I'd rather be out in the front line of the revolution than hiding in a closet."[70] The call for such a revolution is not without precedent among Chicanos. In *Yo Soy Joaquin* Gonzales argues that Chicanos have a long tradition of revolution.[71] In that poem he described the coming Chicano revolution:

> And now the trumpet sounds,
> the music of the people stirs the
>   revolution.
> Like a sleepy giant it slowly
> rears its head
> to the sound of
>   tramping feet
>   clamoring voices

> mariachi strains
> fiery tequila explosions
> the smell of chile verde and
> soft brown eyes of expectation for a
> better life.
> And in the fertile farmlands,
> the barren plains,
> the mountain villages,
> smoke-smeared cities,
> we start to MOVE.[72]

The revolutionary movement truly would begin, Gonzales continued, once the Chicano leaders threw off their present confusion and found clear direction. When Chicanos acquired the necessary cultural nationalism and pride in heritage, young Chicanos would lead the movement to its goals through political solutions such as those provided by the Crusade for Justice.

Nationalism

The first obstacle to surmount was divisiveness in the Chicano community. Gonzales proclaimed that a "national consciousness is very important."[73] Although each locality had to solve its unique problems, a national movement could solve problems common to all Chicanos. To Gonzales,

the key common denominator is nationalism. When I talk about nationalism, some people run around in their intellectual bags, and say this is reverse racism. . . . Nationalism becomes la familia. Nationalism comes first out of the family, then into tribalism, and then into the alliances that are necessary to lift the burden of all suppressed humanity.[74]

In his view nationalism was not a sign of racism but rather a positive means of changing people's attitudes: "You can't love someone else when you don't respect or love yourself. . . . People are starting to analyze and recognize themselves."[75] Nationalism thus became a tool for organization, not a weapon for racism: "The guys that say we're organizing that way are probably the most nationalistic or white racist there are, but it bothers them for us to organize."[76]

Nationalism for Chicanos required that they create and inhabit the nation of Aztlan, for as Gonzales declared: "Aztlan is a spiritual call for self-determination. It has become a program to inspire and to commit all Chicanos to start to develop their own leadership, make their own decisions, take over their own communities and liberate the institutions which direct and control our lives."[77]

Like other major Chicano leaders, Gonzales did not clearly define what he meant by Aztlan. The term can assume a variety of meanings:

Historians say that Aztlan was the land from which the Aztecs began the long wandering that finally led them to Mexico City. According to some, this land was located in the northwestern part of Mexico—today, the Southwest of the United States. Others say that Aztlan may well have been "the place of the reeds," an ancient marsh—now desert—near Kanab, Utah. And according to still others, the word "Aztlan" in the Nahuatl language simply means . . . "the place beyond." This of course could mean almost any place and that is very appropriate to our new concept of Aztlan. It means that Aztlan may be a myth or it may be a real place, but it always stands for the idea of a homeland, of freedom from that which we are not, of reclaiming what we are.[78]

Perhaps Gonzales's fullest description of Aztlan was in El Plan de Aztlan:

Brotherhood unites us, and love for our brothers makes us a people whose time has come and who struggles against the foreigner Gabacho who exploits our riches and destroys our culture. With our heart in our hands and our hands in the soil, we declare the independence of our *mestizo* nation. We are a bronze people with a bronze culture. Before the world, before all of North America, before all our brothers in the bronze continent, we are a nation, we are a union of free pueblos, we are AZTLAN.[79]

Pride in Heritage

A central piece in Gonzales's rhetorical vision and a key to developing nationalism was the need for Chicanos to know their heritage and take pride in it. This heritage, which was being destroyed by the Anglo school system wherein Chicano students were being "infected with cancer and having their self-image destroyed," would be inculcated in the newly created schools at the Crusade for Justice.[80] Gonzales recognized, however, that not all Mexican-American students were able to attend schools operated by Chicanos. He therefore advocated changes in the public schools. In a speech before the Denver school board he demanded the teaching of Chicano history, culture, language, and contributions of Chicanos to the nation. He called for bilingual education; teachers who lived in the neighborhoods where they taught; the preservation of Chicano values, culture, and family life; and an end to the policy of encouraging Chicanos to enter the armed forces. The Anglo system must also be explained to the young:

We're going to teach them about this system, the economic problems. We're going to teach them about the legislation that is rotten and corrupt. We're going to teach them about the politicians that are using our people. We're going to teach them about the welfare system that perpetuates itself in order to keep people in bondage. We're going to teach them about the different government finance programs that take our best leadership.[81]

Such learning would teach the lesson that

We are still not completely absorbed by this society. By this monstrous new creation. I don't call it a modern culture 'cause there is no culture in this society. It's just a society. The values are all mixed up and corrupted because you contradict or rather that society contradicts everything it does.[82]

This new curriculum emphasized the positive aspects of Chicano heritage. Gonzales's proclamation "The Plan of The Barrio" included the "demand that from kindergarten through college, Spanish be the first language and English the second language and the textbooks to be rewritten to emphasize the heritage and the contributions of the Mexican American or Indo-Hispano in the building of the Southwest."[83] Students would discover that "Chicano history predates Plymouth Rock and Jamestown. Chicanos don't come from the East Coast. . . . When we start relating to what we are and where we come from we will start becoming proud of ourselves."[84] Young Chicanos needed to realize that they had heroes of Indian background, like Emiliano Zapata and Benito Juarez.[85]

The often ignored and maligned Indian roots became an exalted part of the new Chicano:

> The Indian has endured and still
> emerged the winner,
> the Mestizo must yet overcome
>   and the gachupin will just ignore.
> I look at myself
> and see part of me
> who rejects my father and my mother
> and dissolves into the melting pot
> to disappear in shame.[86]

The preeminence of the Indian heritage was made particularly clear in Gonzales's poetry:

> I am Cuauhtemoc,
> proud and noble,
>   leader of men,
> king of an empire
> civilized beyond the dreams
>   of the gachupin Cortes,
> who also is the blood,
>   the image of myself.
> I am the Maya prince.
> I am Nezahualcoyotl,
> great leader of the Chichimecas.
> I am the sword and flame of Cortes
>   the despot.
>   And
> I am the eagle and serpent of
> the Aztec Civilization.[87]

Once they were proud of their heritage, Chicanos would accept other aspects of their past, a past which revealed a courageous capacity for survival against all odds:

I have endured in the rugged mountains
    of the country.
I have survived the toils and slavery
    of the fields.
            I have existed
in the barrios of the city
in the suburbs of bigotry
in the mines of social snobbery
in the prisons of dejection
in the muck of exploitation
and
in the fierce heat of racial hatred.[88]

This tenacity kept alive a special person, both Indian and Spanish in heritage, the Chicano:

            ¡La Raza!
    ¡Mejicano!
        ¡Español!
        ¡Latino!
        ¡Hispano!
        ¡Chicano!
or whatever I call myself,
                I look the same
                I feel the same
    I cry
            and
                sing the same.
I am the masses of my people and
I refuse to be absorbed
            I am Joaquin
The odds are great
but my spirit is strong,
                    my faith unbreakable,
                    my blood is pure.
I am Aztec prince and Christian Christ.
            I SHALL ENDURE
            I WILL ENDURE.[89]

The Future

Gonzales believed that young Chicanos must finish the battle that he started: "Our best investment is in our young, since they will have to carry our struggle into the next century. I doubt if we can solve our complex problems with the Gringo within a few years."[90] Moreover, young militants had been fighting the Anglo for the shortest period of time, were the least likely to have been defeated, and were "starting to realize that they are not a conquered people."[91]

The primary role of older leaders like Gonzales was to instill nationalism in the young. Once a young Chicano found pride and began "identifying with who he is, what he is and what his purpose in life is," he or she would discover Chicano identity.[92] If this young Chicano could be kept within the community and not be co-opted by the Anglos, the Chicano movement would become the "biggest, strongest and most powerful movement in the nation."[93]

Self-identification, however, was only one step toward a series of long-range goals. For while the "cultural renaissance" was initiated to create "cultural awareness" and a "positive image of ourselves" through Chicano studies at universities and through other means, Gonzales pointed out that Chicanos must "escalate" the battle into areas "like economic development and political philosophy."[94]

Politics

Beginning with the fact that Chicanos constituted a large and rapidly growing population, Gonzales reasoned that his people could unite to form a powerful political force. Drawing on his past political experience, Gonzales decided that a Chicano political party could best "break down regionalism" among Chicanos.[95] He predicted that everyone "who runs in the different areas will be expressing the philosophy of a political party, the philosophy of Aztlan, the philosophy of the nation." Because "nationalism transcends all political beliefs," he concluded, "we are concerned with being a Chicano party first, being Chicano first, and everything else secondary. If you are a Catholic, you are a Catholic. . . . But the one common denominator . . . we are Chicano."[96]

For Chicanos to become a political force required rejection of the Democratic and Republican parties, "an animal with two heads eating out of the same trough, that sits on the same board of directors of the banks and corporations, that shares in the same industries that make dollars and profits off war. To fight this thing, you look for the tools."[97] These tools were the philosophy and ideology of the new political party, La Raza Unida, whose major purpose was to "expose issues and to educate people into the movement."[98] Meier and Rivera describe La Raza Unida:

Although basically a political party, La Raza Unida is also something more. . . . Its leaders envision it as an ethnic institution that will break the cycle of Chicano repression by organizing community classes as well as political groups, by launching massive registration drives, by providing draft counseling, and by supplying economic expertise and support to Chicano chambers of commerce. They see La Raza Unida not as a means of achieving power in order to enter the mainstream of American society but as a way of safeguarding their bicultural and bilingual uniqueness.[99]

The creation of La Raza Unida did not mean, however, that Chicanos should vote for someone simply because he or she was of Mexican descent. Gonzales noted that frequently Chicanos voted for someone because of a surname: "You realize that if . . . any . . . popular figure in the Mexicano scene decides to run . . . as popular as he is, then out of nationalism we would vote for an idiot. . . . And we have elected too many idiots in the past out of nationalism."[100] Instead of mindless voting, Chicanos must support political causes favorable to the Chicano people and reject "those people who confuse and mislead gullible members of our Raza. I can no longer bargain with despotic Government representatives," Gonzales warned. "I want no type of alignment with political prostitutes; I have no intention of creating reaction for the profitable benefit of professional program managers."[101]

Once united culturally and politically, Chicanos could channel the energy formerly spent fighting each other into the struggle against the Anglo. Gonzales recommended that the Chicano movement could redirect people's "attitudes and their directions towards the real revolutionary thought instead of going outside and showing their *machismo* and blasting each other in some alley, on some street because they're mad and mean and they know there's revolution in them but they don't know where to go."[102] With unity and direction, Chicanos could acquire power and self-respect. As Gonzales reminded his listeners, "the Anglo respects you only when you have power and respect yourself."[103]

Crusade for Justice

To reach Aztlan, Gonzales exhorted Chicanos to lead their own revolution: "We will make our own mistakes. And if they're wrong we'll suffer from them."[104] The past practice of Anglo control over the Chicano protest was well intentioned but unproductive: "They're the Big Brother that hands down the ideas. They come into our communities to try and organize us, and they create more problems than if they stayed out of our community, went back to their middle-class society and taught them something about living, something about life."[105] The Chicanos asked to be left alone:

Economic control of our lives and our communities can only come about by driving the exploiter out of our communities, our *pueblos*, and our lands and by controlling and developing our own talents, sweat, and resources. Cultural background and values which ignore materialism and embrace humanism will contribute to the act of cooperative buying and the distribution of resources and production to sustain an economic base for healthy growth and development. Lands rightfully ours will be fought for and defended.[106]

Gonzales founded the Crusade for Justice as a vehicle to unify Chicanos, train leaders, and control mass actions in the community. This organization protected Chicanos from the "corruption of life by gringo values—a corruption which has produced the 'generation gap' as well as a cultural gap. Of course, different age groups have different interests. But at the Crusade they have a basic unity of purpose in life: to live selflessly for the good of our people."[107] At the Crusade, where meetings were described as being like a "big family gathering with people coming together to present a united front on an issue," decisions were made by consensus of its membership.[108]

CONCLUSION

Relying on his experiences in both urban and rural worlds, Rodolfo "Corky" Gonzales created a discourse that unified all Chicanos. He particularly appealed to rural Chicanos who were forced off the land and into urban settings. His Crusade for Justice was established to solve specific problems for Chicanos in the urban barrio of Denver.

Gonzales's barrio background, in combination with his persona as a defiant ex-boxer who had succeeded in and then rejected the Establishment, prepared him well to address urban youth, the backbone of the movement. Speaking in the inspirational language of youthful idealism, he attracted an audience of the future. Chicanos, it must be remembered, constituted a young demographic group with a reproduction rate double that of the general society, and 80 percent of them lived in the cities in the late 1960s.[109]

Gonzales employed a militant rhetoric—perhaps the most militant of any of the leaders discussed in this book. This militance was not confined to public speeches, and his most powerful messages were in written form: poetry, plays, and proclamations. The popularity and influence of his writings illustrate the power of the written word in the Chicano movement.

In his discourse Gonzales created a vision of Chicanos who were oppressed in many ways by Anglos but who had untapped political power to control their own destiny. Because he first popularized the potent ideas of Chicano nationalism and Aztlan, ideas which other activists subsequently included in their discourse, he has been credited with making the greatest contribution "to the spirit, ideology and philosophy of the Chicano movement."[110] Indeed, the Denver poet became the "leading apostle for Chicano nationalism," a primary source of Chicano unity and self-identification.[111]

NOTES

1. "Corky speaks con su Corazon," *La Verdad*, June 1969, p. 14.
2. Rudolph O. de la Garza and Rowena Rivera, "The Socio-Political World of the Chicano: A Comparative Analysis of Social Scientific and

Literary Perspectives," in *Minority Language and Literature, Retrospective and Perspective*, ed. Dexter Fisher (New York: Modern Language Association, 1977), pp. 50–51, quoted in Michael Victor Sedano, "Chicanismo: A Rhetorical Analysis of Themes and Images of Selected Poetry from the Chicano Movement," *Western Journal of Speech Communication* 44 (1980), p. 178.

3. For a complete text of the poem, see Rodolfo Gonzales, *I Am Joaquin* (New York: Bantam Books, 1972). Gonzales is also the author of *The Revolutionist* and *A Cross for Maclovio* (plays), *Sol, Lagrimas, Sangre* (poetry), and was the publisher of a newspaper. The poem also has been made into a movie.

4. Christine Marin, *A Spokesman of the Mexican American Movement: Rodolfo "Corky" Gonzales and the Fight for Chicano Liberation, 1966–1972* (San Francisco: R and E Research Associates, 1977), pp. 1–2. Marin provides an excellent summary of the events in Gonzales's life on pages 1–5.

5. Stan Steiner, *La Raza: The Mexican Americans* (New York: Harper and Row, 1969), p. 380. In his book Steiner includes a chapter on Gonzales entitled "The Poet in the Boxing Ring." See pages 378–392.

6. Quoted in Steiner, p. 380.

7. Ibid.

8. Gonzales, *I Am Joaquin*, p. 60.

9. Quoted in Steiner, p. 381.

10. Steiner, p. 381.

11. Marin, p. 3.

12. Quoted in Marin, p. 3.

13. Marin, p. 3; Steiner, pp. 381–382.

14. Quoted in Steiner, p. 383.

15. Matt Meier and Feliciano Rivera, *The Chicanos: A History of Mexican-Americans* (New York: Hill and Wang, 1972), p. 274.

16. Meier and Rivera, p. 275.

17. Marin, p. 7. At the march Gonzales was unable to work well with black leaders.

18. Froben Lozada and Antonio Camejo, "A Militant Interview: Corky Gonzales on the Chicano Liberation Fight," *The Militant*, 9 May 1969, p. 10, quoted in Marin, p. 12.

19. Marin, p. 15.

20. Ibid., p. 13. For a copy of the plan, see Marin, pp. 35–37.

21. Quoted in Marin, p. 37.

22. Marin describes the election on pages 27–31.

23. Gonzales, *I Am Joaquin*, pp. 2–3.

24. Rodolfo Acuña, *Occupied America: The Chicano's Struggle Toward*

Liberation (San Francisco: Canfield Press, 1972), p. 241. Soon after the poem was written, *La Raza* announced: " 'I Am Joaquin' is fast becoming a legend in the Southwest. The version that came to our hands was being passed from hand to hand on a 3rd carbon copy, read aloud and recited in bars and cantinas of the lower Rio Grande Valley. 'I Am Joaquin' is also a poem of independence. Independence of the soul of a people and expression of a determination to fight to the end for Freedom and Justice." See "I Am Joaquin," *La Raza*, 16 September 1967, p. 4.

25. Quoted in Marin, p. 36.

26. Gonzales, *I Am Joaquin*, p. 1.

27. Rodolfo "Corky" Gonzales, "Why a Chicano Party?" *La Raza!* (New York: Pathfinder Press, 1970), p. 9.

28. Gonzales, *I Am Joaquin*, p. 6.

29. Quoted in Homer Bigart, "Mexican-Americans Take on New Militancy in Struggle for Identity," *New York Times*, 20 April 1969, p. 54.

30. "I Am Joaquin," p. 5.

31. Quoted in Martin Waldron, "New Mexican-American Party Hails Growth of Brown Power," *New York Times*, 4 September 1972, p. 16.

32. "Corky In L.A.," *La Raza*, 15 November 1967, p. 6.

33. Rodolfo Gonzales, "Social Revolution in the Southwest," a speech at the University of Colorado, Denver, 20 November 1967, in Robert Tice, "Rhetoric of La Raza," unpublished manuscript, Chicano Studies Collection, Arizona State University, Tempe, Arizona, 1971, p. 2, appendix.

34. Gonzales, "Why a Chicano Party?" p. 10.

35. Ibid.

36. Gonzales, "Social Revolution in the Southwest," p. 2.

37. Quoted in Marin, p. 37.

38. Marin, p. 2.

39. "Corky in L.A.," p. 6.

40. Ibid.

41. "Corky speaks con su Corazon," p. 14.

42. Gonzales, *I Am Joaquin*, p. 9.

43. Gonzales, "Social Revolution in the Southwest," p. 6.

44. Gonzales, *I Am Joaquin*, p. 51.

45. "The Poor People's March," *La Raza*, 10 July 1968, p. 8.

46. Gonzales, "Social Revolution in the Southwest," p. 5.

47. Gonzales, *I Am Joaquin*, p. 62.

48. Quoted in Marin, p. 36.

49. Marin describes such confrontations, pp. 24–26.

50. "Colorado Raza Unida Spokesman: The People Are Starting to Move Collectively," *The Militant*, 4 December 1970, p. 11.

51. Quoted in Bigart, p. 54.

52. "The Poor People's March," p. 8.

53. Gonzales, "Social Revolution in the Southwest," p. 5.

54. Ibid.

55. Ibid., p. 13.

56. "The Poor People's March," p. 8.

57. Gonzales, *I Am Joaquin*, p. 66.

58. Elizabeth Sutherland Martinez and Enriqueta Longeaux y Vasquez, *Viva La Raza! The Struggle of the Mexican-American People* (Garden City: Doubleday and Co., 1974), p. 235.

59. Ibid., p. 238.

60. Ibid., p. 235.

61. Gonzales, "Social Revolution in the Southwest," pp. 17–18.

62. Quoted in Marin, p. 36.

63. Gonzales, "Why a Chicano Party?" p. 2.

64. Ibid.

65. Gonzales, *I Am Joaquin*, p. 20.

66. Ibid., p. 70.

67. Quoted in Marin, p. 36.

68. "I Am Joaquin," p. 5.

69. Quoted in Augustin Garza, "Interview with Rodolfo 'Corky' Gonzales," *La Voz del Pueblo*, May 1971, p. 5.

70. Gonzales, "Social Revolution in the Southwest," p. 20.

71. For example, see Gonzales, *I Am Joaquin*, p. 25.

72. Ibid., pp. 93 and 96.

73. Rodolfo "Corky" Gonzales, "The Need for a Chicano Political Party," *The Militant*, 17 April 1970, p. 9.

74. Gonzales, "Why a Chicano Party?" p. 9.

75. Quoted in Garza, p. 4.

76. Ibid.

77. "Corky speaks con su Corazon," p. 14.

78. Martinez and Vasquez, p. 252.

79. Quoted in Marin, p. 35.

80. "Colorado Raza Unida Spokesman," p. 11.

81. Gonzales, "Social Revolution in the Southwest," pp. 14–15.

82. Ibid., p. 16.

83. Gonzales quoted in Steiner, p. 388.

84. Gonzales quoted in *Colorado Daily*, May 1, 1970, quoted in Carlos Larralde, *Mexican-American Movements and Leaders* (Los Alamitos, Calif.: Hwong Publishing, 1976), p. 202.

85. Ramon Eduardo Ruiz, "Another Defector from the Gringo World," *New Republic*, 27 July 1968, p. 11.

86. Gonzales, *I Am Joaquin*, p. 52.

87. Ibid., p. 16.

88. Ibid., p. 86.

89. Ibid., pp. 98–100.

90. Gonzales quoted in *Colorado Daily*, May 1, 1970, quoted in Larralde, p. 201.

91. Gonzales, "Social Revolution in the Southwest," p. 6.

92. Ibid., p. 20.

93. Gonzales quoted in *Colorado Daily*, May 1, 1970, quoted in Larralde, p. 202.

94. "Colorado Raza Unida Spokesman," p. 10.

95. Gonzales, "The Need for a Chicano Political Party," p. 9.

96. Ibid.

97. Gonzales, "Why a Chicano Party?" p. 10.

98. Gonzales quoted in Garza, p. 4.

99. Meier and Rivera, p. 277.

100. Gonzales, "Why a Chicano Party?" p. 10.

101. Rodolfo "Corky" Gonzales, "Corky's Letter to Tijerina," *El Grito Del Norte*, November 1972, p. 9.

102. Gonzales, "Social Revolution in the Southwest," p. 14.

103. Quoted in Steiner, p. 386.

104. Gonzales, "Social Revolution in the Southwest," p. 17.

105. Ibid., p. 7.

106. "El Plan de Aztlan" quoted in Marin, p. 36.

107. Martinez and Vasquez, p. 246.

108. Ibid.

109. Matt S. Meier and Feliciano Rivera, "Afterward: The Future," in *Readings in La Raza: The Twentieth Century*, ed. Meier and Rivera (New York: Hill and Wang, 1974), p. 275.

110. Maurilio Vigil, *Chicano Politics* (Washington, D.C.: University Press of America, 1968), p. 284.

111. Tony Castro, *Chicano Power: The Emergence of Mexican America* (New York: Saturday Review Press, 1974), p. 222.

5

Creating a Nation in Spirit and Reality: The Rhetoric of Jose Angel Gutierrez

In their book *The Chicano Political Experience: Three Perspectives*, F. Chris Garcia and Rudolph O. de la Garza described the 1969 Chicano takeover of political power in Crystal City, Texas, as "a model for Chicano activists everywhere."[1] Garcia and de la Garza credited the leader of that movement, Jose Angel Gutierrez, with using the Anglo's own political system to defeat the Establishment. Recognizing the "ever-present factor" of racism in Texas politics, Gutierrez "tapped this bitterness and converted it into a political resource."[2] "The Crystal City takeover cannot be construed as merely a political victory," concluded Garcia and de la Garza:

It was and is far more than that, and Gutierrez and others do their best to insure that the community understands this greater meaning. It was above all a move toward freedom, toward the right to be *Mexicano*, to speak Spanish, to attend school, to live with dignity. It was not, therefore, a simple political contest but instead a battle by Chicanos to overthrow their oppressors.[3]

This chapter will focus on Gutierrez the individual and on his rhetorical tactics in Crystal City. We will first detail the events of Gutierrez's life and then delineate the discourse he used to achieve his goals. Gutierrez possessed the proper background to achieve successes in his battle for the Chicano cause. Accordingly, this chapter will begin with an examination of events in his life and then proceed to an analysis of the discourse he employed to reach his goals.

GUTIERREZ'S TRAINING AND BACKGROUND

Jose Angel Gutierrez was born in Crystal City, Texas, in 1944. His father was a medical doctor, and his family did not suffer the same degree of poverty as many other Mexican-American families in the community. In high school Gutierrez was elected president of the student body, won honors as a championship debater,[4] and, in general, "conducted himself in a manner many Anglos found commendable and reassuring."[5] He "had been the kind of student Anglos liked to point to as an example of how a bright and ambitious Mexican-American could get ahead."[6] Despite his accomplishments, he remembered suffering from discrimination which sometimes took subtle forms, as revealed in later conversations with Crystal City Anglos who almost always included stories of how some dedicated Anglo teachers had driven him to far-off public speaking and debating engagements "in their own cars ... with their own gas."[7] Years later, Gutierrez recalled the subtle discrimination as well as the valuable training he received in debate.

I was always told that I was different because I was good and it never dawned on me that it was because I was Chicano. I had a separate motel room, I would ride separately in a car with the coach. I didn't realize that and in competition I remember knowing that I was the only Chicano there, but not necessarily feeling it until we had some judges' comments. The comments always applied to me; there were problems with enunciation, accents—those were the sorts of things that at that time were handicaps to Chicanos. . . . I think that the training that the coaches gave me, always drilling me in terms of speech style, the mechanics of speaking, to be clear, to be slow, to be forceful, the intonation—I remember going through all that . . . . The poise that one acquires through experience, not having fear of audiences, being sure of your abilities, all that comes from experience and my experience began when I was sixteen or fifteen years old.[8]

Gutierrez left Crystal City to attend St. Mary's University in San Antonio, where he began to formulate his ideas on political action. In 1963 he worked in a successful campaign to elect five Mexican-Americans to the city council of Crystal City, a town where Anglos had traditionally dominated politics, though Mexican-Americans comprised a majority of the population. Gutierrez expressed the need for change in a speech during the campaign: "They say there is no discrimination, but we only have to look around to know the truth. We look at the schools . . . the house we live in . . . the few opportunities . . . the dirt in the streets . . . and we know."[9] In his mind the 1963 election was a "revolution":

Never in the history of the State of Texas had such a significant event taken place. It was historic because for the first time, Mexican-Americans had used the political process to exercise their desire to change the existing political and social conditions. Never before had this minority group successfully drawn attention to their plight or ever succeeded in radically affecting social change. Since this event, numerous Mexican-American organizations and groups have engaged in patterns of concerted social action.[10]

During the 1963 campaign Gutierrez claimed he was physically beaten by Texas Rangers. His resulting hatred of the Rangers frequently surfaced in his public address. Years later, for example, he declared: "I guarantee you that the Rangers are not getting more than six feet from me . . . . And if he makes any funny moves, it is either me or him . . . . I'm not looking for a fight but I am not going to run away from one."[11]

In 1967, while a student at St. Mary's University in San Antonio, Gutierrez and four other young Chicanos founded the Mexican-American Youth Organization (MAYO) to meet "a need for an active and aggressive organization that would offer the Mexican-American youth a vehicle with which to effect meaningful social change."[12] The founders maintained that traditional Mexican-American organizations were not recruiting young Mexican-Americans, developing leadership expertise among them, or engaging in direct-action projects and community organization. Composed of young militants whose education and

" 'Anglicization' gave them greater confidence in confrontation with the gringo,"[13] MAYO formulated goals which included "the forming of third parties separate from either the Democrats or the Republicans, gaining control of the educational systems in Chicano communities, and ending Anglo economic domination by the development of their own business and cooperatives."[14]

John Staples Shockley has pointed out that "this phenomenon of needing to have the most educated and acculturated members of the Mexican-American community—those who understand the system best—become the backbone of the leadership, has produced a number of ironies."[15] One of the greatest was that the leadership was more "anglicized" than most members of the Mexican-American community. Another irony was that many Chicanos argued "for their 'rights' as American rather than Mexican citizens. For a definite segment of the Mexican-American population, their view of themselves as Americans seems itself to have been a radicalizing influence."[16]

After receiving an M.A. degree in political science in 1969, Gutierrez returned to Crystal City and began organizing Mexican-Americans in the community. His return was an example of a common phenomenon of the time: educated Chicanos returned to their community to organize their people. As Gutierrez concluded: "There is no longer concern for earning the title 'All-American Boy' or 'Good Boy.' We're not going to accept anything less than complete liberation and complete control of the resources and the government and the educational institutions that are in this area. And this is going to make for a very radical transition."[17]

Because Gutierrez was well known in the community, "charges of atheism, communism, and extremism—while they need to be answered—would not be an insurmountable barrier."[18] He explained: "They tried the 'outside agitator' bit on me but it didn't work because I was born in Crystal City. So they changed gears. Then they tried the 'communist' one for a while—until they found out I was in the U.S. Army Reserves. . . . Then somewhere they dug up my 'kill a gringo' thing . . . when I said I would kill a gringo in self-defense if I were attacked."[19]

Gutierrez proved to be a skillful organizer. When Chicano students at Crystal City High School rebelled against racial practices at the school, he worked behind the scenes to help orchestrate those events into changes in the school and eventually the whole community.[20] He faced problems of animating Chicanos on educational issues: "Since our arrival in Cristal one of the most difficult tasks has been to transfer the opinions and beliefs of my companions into actions, particularly when discussion centered around the students' problems."[21] Discovering that men in the community seemed unwilling to act on school issues, he developed a tactic based on the "psychology of a beer joint crowd."[22] He described this tactic:

Julian Salas, Nano Serna and I went to drink beer at several bars. At each and every one we'd raise the issue of the impending Board meeting. We'd talk about the specific issues. We talked about the guts of the students. We talked about the general conditions in which Chicanos found themselves. Eventually, others would echo our remarks. At the point that the predominant conversation was the school trouble, we left for another bar.

That night our agenda was the same. Nano, Julian and I made our rounds again . . . . A qualitative difference in their remarks was quickly noted. The objectivity and reflection on the issues that had been demonstrated that afternoon was gone. The beer had loosened their inhibitions . . . . Commitments were made in loud voices of boast and arrogance to take on all the gringos. As we left, the beertalk was getting into violence and bravado.[23]

Gutierrez's talking attracted men into his active campaign, and soon the solidarity and power of the community increased. When extensive changes occurred in the schools, he turned his attention to the larger community.[24]

At this period in his life Gutierrez was "an articulate, self-confident, well-educated Chicano with a very definite program ready to be implemented."[25] To implement that program, he helped found the Chicano political party, La Raza Unida, in 1970. Two immediate goals of La Raza Unida were "to show Anglo politicians that Chicanos were no longer dependent on them and to make the Chicano community aware of the possibilities to make changes and improve its conditions through the development and use of alternative strategies."[26] In 1970 La Raza Unida dramatically demonstrated that it had learned to use the political process. It elected several members to the Crystal City Council and a majority of the local school board—which selected Gutierrez as board president. A further indication of La Raza's political success was the election of Gutierrez as a county judge in 1974.[27]

Gutierrez understood the political system and how an activist could succeed in it. In his M.A. thesis and his later writings, he examined how Chicanos could unite effectively to challenge Anglo-dominated politics. In effect, he became a theorist/activist of Chicano mass action. Ricardo Sanchez described him as "an activist, and quite possibly the mentor to revolutionary political theory and doctrine in the Chicano community."[28] Gutierrez wrote *A Gringo Manual on How to Handle Mexicans* to share his knowledge of the Anglo system and how to defeat it: "This book," he announced, "is a limited manual on how to deal with a racist, imperialist, colonialized society of white people."[29] Outlining his theory of organizing, he related: "You don't impose an issue on the community, the community raises the issue. Organizing really mobilizes what is there. People should be presented with the problem and the solution. A good organizer knows the solutions before he tackles the problems."[30]

GUTIERREZ'S PUBLIC ADDRESS

While Gutierrez's education gave him a theoretical basis for Chicano mass action, his direct experience in practical politics taught him how to express his ideas to activate his listeners. One challenge he faced was the need of an accepted term that would unite the Mexican-American community. Encountering difficulty in finding a term that would fit its variegated culture and society, the group had referred to itself by a number of labels, including Mexican, Mexican-American, Spanish, Spanish-American, and Hispanic. In his speeches and writings Gutierrez offered the term *Chicano* as a cohesive label. The origins and even the definition of the term *Chicano* are difficult to trace, however, even for Gutierrez:

Some people say that it came from the word *chicaro*, you know which is pigpen. Other people think it comes from Chiquita bananas . . . and there is one that says it was shortened from *mexicano*. So it doesn't make any difference...which one you want to take. That's not the point. The thing is that back in the early fifties a lot of Mexicanos who were different in terms of their lifestyles, in terms of their language, in terms of their aspirations were called *pachuco*. And these guys were given the name because they were different from the regular Mexican. And now this same idea is applying to those different Mexicans who are very militant, who are very aggressive in pursuit of what they deem to be their self-interest. So people get concerned because they don't know what it is that we're all excited about.[31]

In a speech at the University of Texas, Gutierrez gave the meaning of the term *Chicano*: "We're really talking about two things here—the definition and we're talking about identity or trying to identify what is what.... I can't think of a better description than to just...give a flat answer that we know what a Chicano is because we are one."[32]

Chicano was the dominant but not the only major term Gutierrez used in his attempt to create solidarity within the community. He argued that a "social movement must have a vision, a belief in the possibility of a different state of affairs."[33] This vision coalesced into what he called the creation of Aztlan.

Aztlan may be defined as "the mythical northern kingdom of the Aztecs, now the southwestern United States."[34] The term linked Chicanos to their Indian ancestors and stressed the importance of land in the Mexican-American community. In Gutierrez's message, land was vital to Chicanos in South Texas: "The land is owned by a few people and the ownership of such great holdings in an agrarian area is extremely important. Those who own the land virtually possess and control the wealth. Land is synonymous with wealth."[35]

Gutierrez related the broad consequences of the loss of land by Mexican-Americans:

When our lands in Aztlan (the Southwest to you) were made United States Government property, our people remained devout, culturally conservative and proud and loyal to the new government.... We had hoped that we would be made a part of America with all the rights and privileges other Americans enjoy. But that was a foolish dream because today America continues to exact more from us than we are able to give.[36]

To many, Aztlan was an ideal; to others, it was a physical reality in the future. In either case Aztlan served as a powerful image for building solidarity in the community. Gutierrez contended that "currently in the Chicano movement there is some talk about creating Aztlan, and right now it is in the psychological stage. We feel that we already are a nation in spirit and in reality."[37] He promised that his followers would work to achieve Aztlan.

A third powerful term was the title of the Chicano political party, La Raza Unida (the united people). That name indicated that all members of the Mexican-American community could unite to fight politically for their rights. A similar powerful term was La Raza (the people). Again, the term showed that the group should become one against a common foe.

Gutierrez's discourse also contained terms that referred specifically to ethnic origin, religion, color, or race. He referred to the Catholic Church because of its importance in the Mexican-American community,[38] to "Brown" as a reference to skin color in the community,[39] and to culture, heritage, and land to focus on the uniqueness of the culture. These terms identified him with the rest of the Mexican-American community and called attention to its uniqueness.

Solidarity in the Chicano community was developed further by applying negative terms to depict the Anglo as the ultimate devil. Gutierrez urged Chicanos to unite against that devil, whom he referred to as bigoted, un-American, racist, animalistic, foreigner, thief, exploiter, barbarian, white supremacist, clever (in a negative sense), and full of hatred. Texas Rangers and the Alamo symbolized the terrible treatment of Chicanos in Texas, and metaphors such as "cannon fodder" referred to the treatment of Chicanos by gringos. Gutierrez declared: "our devil has pale skin and blue eyes";[40] "Gringo is an attitude . . . . If you ask a Chicano what a Gringo is, he knows";[41] the Gringo is hated because he has "divided us, robbed us, repressed us."[42] He elaborated on this theme: "You can begin to understand how to define the word 'gringo,' which seems to be such a problem all the time. It is funny, because the Mexicano knows what a gringo is. It's the gringos themselves that are worried about what the hell it is. . . . The basic idea in using the word 'gringo' is that it means 'foreigner.' "[43]

Not only did Gutierrez attempt to create solidarity in the community through his use of positive terms for Chicanos and negative ones for Anglos, but he also tried to create a new reality for Chicanos by contrasting the ways Anglos had structured reality for Chicanos with the new image and reality he sought to create. He explained that the Anglo version of Chicano history wrongly omitted the Chicanos' history of dissent, falsely equated brownness with inferiority, and insidiously distorted their cultural heritage. According to him, "The gravest sin to date committed by the media, social scientists, businessmen and government agents is the creation of the myth that la raza is silent, permissive and without protest."[44] On the contrary, he argued, Chicanos have been active protestors: "The resistance movement had its origin in the Cart Wars of Juan Cortina. Later it was carried on by Joaquin Murietta, El Plan de San Diego, Gregorio Cortez, the Vaquero Strikes (1915), Zoot Suit Riots (1942), Reies Tijerina and the Alianza (1968), and, presently, the Chicano Liberation Front."[45]

The "myth" of passiveness originated when Anglos defeated older generations of Mexican-Americans. As Gutierrez stated: "Our parents have been made weak. Through the years they have learned to accept humiliation and reproach. They bitterly got accustomed to letting the gringo have his way."[46] Reviewing politics, he lamented that the Anglo Establishment had crushed Mexican-American leaders: "Mexican-American leaders who have worked with the Establishment have conformed to the norms of the power structure. The youth feel that these leaders leave as representatives of the Mexican-Americans and return as representatives to the Mexican-Americans."[47]

Such suppression of Chicanos rested on the Anglo's suspicion that "even native-born Americans of Mexican descent are not very good Americans and are always suspect."[48] The suspicion grew out of the Chicano status as colonized Americans, and even a "thousand degrees from Harvard and speaking flawless English will not change our status as colonial subjects."[49] According to Gutierrez, Chicanos believed that they were maintained as colonial subjects because of their skin color. He reasoned that "La Raza is the affirmation of the most basic ingredient of our personality, the brownhood of our Indian ancestors wedded to all the other skin colors of mankind . . . . But in a color-mad society, the sin of our coloration can be expiated only by exceptional achievement and successful imitation of the White Man who controls every institution of society."[50] To Gutierrez, the Mexican-American's history and brownness created

somewhat of a bastard community in that we are not Mexicans from Mexico; we are not Americans in terms of treatment and in terms of things that we receive. Consequently, we get very demanding and very militant about what it is that we want. Because our land—this part here and throughout the Southwest; it is occupied Mexico—is ours."[51]

Scholars had contributed to making Chicanos a "bastard community" by ignoring historical data and depicting brown people as "ahistorical" or as without a history.[52] To remedy the injustice, Chicanos must write their own histories. Not only were Chicanos mistreated by historians, but also the social scientists' research had been biased, stereotypic, racist, and invalid, the creation of "social science fiction."[53] Gutierrez stated that much information on Chicanos "is based on the findings of social scientists who have not only distorted and grossly made and invented new myths. . . . But they also have made us creatures that are apolitical and timeless, somehow just suspended there."[54] He described how this process occurred: "Throughout the literature on Mexican-Americans, statement after statement is found that stereotypes this ethnic group as 'sleepy,' 'awakening,' 'nonachieving,' 'passive,' and countless other generalizations . . . and usually the Mexican-American is viewed, because of his traditional culture, as unorganizable, easily divided, apolitical and emotional."[55] Such myths, maintained Gutierrez, created and supported a false image of Chicanos in both the Anglo and Mexican-American communities:

We're called apathetic, disorganized. We drink beer. Like to make babies. That we fight. That we're slow learners. That we're not . . . as "ambitiously motivated" as an Anglo. That we're weird in terms of art and music. And eveything that is applied to us is really a commentary on society, the Gringo. The problem is not us. The problem is the white society.[56]

Gutierrez's rendition of reality featured Anglos as the cause of the economic problems of Chicanos. He linked Chicano poverty to deprivation in education: "In 1960 the median years of education of persons 25 years of age or older were lower for Mexican-Americans in Texas than for either the Anglo or the Negro. Mexican-Americans had 6.1 years of education contrasted to 11.5 years with the Anglo and 8.1 years for the Negro."[57] This lack of education justified the outrage of Chicanos: "We get very militant and very adamant about the fact that education, the institutions, the teachers, the curriculum is all designed for Gringos. . . . Consequently, we have such a low median grade of attainment."[58]

Inadequate education harmed Chicanos in many ways. "We are the ones" he charged, "who have to join the armed forces of this country in order to get education, in order to get housing, in order to get benefits. So we're used by this country to wage war on people who suffer the same kind of treatment and abuse as we do."[59] Lack of education also created underemployment or unemployment, he pointed out, and Chicanos suffered an unemployment rate at least as high as that of any other minority group; moreover, the Chicanos with jobs were employed mainly as unskilled laborers with little opportunity for advancement.[60] The result was frequent substandard housing, no ownership of land, substandard medical care, and poor nutrition.[61] Lack of influence accompanied these conditions: "Ever see a Mexican buck private? Obviously you have. How about a general? Chicanos seldom are given positions of authority . . . . Chicanos are hired at the bottom rungs of the corporate structure. This way the Gringos can continue in positions of power and control."[62]

To overcome the image created by the past, Gutierrez operated from the start on the theory that the only way to build a movement to give Mexican-Americans some political power in Crystal City would be to shake them from their dependence on Anglos and Anglo values.[63] A first step toward independence from Anglos would result "when you reinforce what's natural in the Chicano community about birthrights" and when you reinforce the Chicano's attitude about self-respect and the music and the food and the architecture, and all the other symbols. . . . And when these things become a part of his life the Chicano—most of the time—will identify with the changes that are being made now they are legitimate and now they are effective and now they are tasting for the first time these kinds of victories."[64]

This reinforcement and new identity required deeds as well as words:

But we need also to be very sincere about our rhetoric. We're talking about La Raza Unida, about the Gringo and so on. It may make us feel good temporarily, but that's not reality, baby. You've got to work and work hard! You've got to help carry the load of others who may be weaker, who may have already pushed so hard and so long that they need some aid.[65]

Assuming that most older Chicanos were defeated by the Anglos, Gutierrez turned to the younger Chicanos—those for whom the Anglo had created reality for the shortest period of time and who therefore were more capable of rejecting that reality. In order to reduce cleavage in the community, however, he reminded listeners that "Chicanos are very strong because they are very together. They help each other."[66] He contended that the young and old understand each other and that "there is no generation gap between Chicanos. In fact, the older a Chicano is the closer together he is with the youth because he has a lifetime of experience of frustration and pain; and the kids are much brighter today, it doesn't take them so long to catch on."[67] Yet he proclaimed: "There is an emergence of a new Mexican-American. These are young people who are militant, adamant, hostile to the Anglo power structure. They identify the Anglo as the root of *all* evil."[68] Once united, young Chicanos could create change. Gutierrez confided, however, that his generation would not be the beneficiary of his efforts: "The young militants of today will not see the fruits of their efforts. Rather, it is the even younger Mexican-Americans, those in their early teens and pre-teen years, who will reap the benefits of this movement."[69]

Gutierrez outlined some very pragmatic goals:

The government must be made more responsible to our needs. Business and industry must be made to relocate in the Southwest . . . . The news media must be made to relate the problems and struggles of la raza. Private money must be made available for education, housing, economic development, and health services. The land in the Southwest must be redistributed to give the poor a much larger share . . . . In short, white Americans must quickly make a commitment to our well-being, for if we are pushed down the scale of human worth, it is a fact that we will resist with all effort.[70]

Concrete economic and political actions would lead to the life Chicanos desired: "We believe that by virtue of birth we're entitled to dignity, to respect, to a free clean environment and the opportunity to make oneself worth something so he can handle his mind or his mouth or whatever talent he possesses to the full development of his talent. And believe strongly also in the preservation of our culture and our conditioning and our folkways and mores."[71]

Although picturing Chicanos as reluctant "to engage in acts of violence," he saw the value of violent actions. "Must we resort to violence in order to gain national publicity?" he asked; "Is it not enough to march hundreds of miles in protest? Or to have hundreds of students arrested, expelled, suspended and jailed for protesting the denial of their right to self-expression, the right to speak Spanish."[72] "A handful of Black militants," he reminded listeners, "can push this country into a panic through rough talk and ominous warnings. Must we also yell and riot in order to get on the list of priorities? Are we to believe that it takes one riot to get a federal grant, one death to produce a Department of Justice investigation and one shooting to gain a minute of time on Walter Cronkite?"[73]

Although ostensibly opposing violence, he argued that threats of violence and a posture of active defiance were sometimes necessary. "From time to time it is necessary to raise that specter," he concluded, "for whatever reasons. One of the reasons is to get attention and that is what publicity is all about. . . . If you get more attention by saying there may come a time when we have to shoot somebody, well, say it."[74] Shockley described Gutierrez as wanting to develop "machismo into an anti-gringo weapon. Gutierrez himself had said earlier that machismo 'is not to walk around getting three or four women pregnant and to drink a lot of beer. Machismo is to take on the Gringo.' "[75]

Perhaps revealing his own machismo, he warned during a news conference: "You can eliminate an individual in various ways. You can certainly kill him but that is not our intent at this moment. You can remove the base of support that he operates from, be it economic, political or social. That is what we intend to do."[76] La Raza Unida, the vehicle for destroying the Anglo's base of support, sought to "eliminate the Gringo through economic, political, or social means."[77] The actions of La Raza Unida, he recounted, were "more than just a slogan . . . . We began organizing and moving in to counter-attack every time the gringo tried to put pressure on the mexicano. Point the finger at him. Expose him for the animal that he is. Bring in the newspapers and the photographers and the tape recorders. Let the world see it."[78] He elaborated on this theme: "We are going to have to devise some pretty ingenious ways of eliminating these gringos. Yet they don't have to be too ingenious. All you have to do is go out there and look around and have a little common sense."[79] He recommended boycotts of stores and other practical economic tactics as one non-violent but economically punishing means of achieving his goals.

La Raza Unida grew out of the needs of the Mexican-American community: "The formation of this party came about because of the critical need for the people to experience justice. It's just like being hungry. You've got to get food in there immediately, otherwise you get nauseous, you get headaches and pains in your stomach."[80] More specifically, he argued that the party was formed because Chicanos occupied no meaningful positions in the other parties. Republicans and Democrats traditionally picked the leadership for Chicanos, and this leader then delivered Chicano votes to the traditional parties. Gutierrez wanted to break out of that traditional way of participating in politics.

Repeating the words of "Corky" Gonzales, Gutierrez saw the Democratic and Republican parties as "a monster with two heads that eats from the same trough."[81] Although directing harsh words at both parties, he focused his wrath on liberals in the Democratic party: "Another lie is the white liberal approach. 'I like Mexican food. Oh, I just love it' . . . . This kind of character is one that cautions you 'Be careful. Don't be a racist in re-verse.' "[82] Liberals who rebutted that their politics had helped Chicanos got this response: "They always love to make you feel bad. And oh, my God, we hate to hurt the feelings of a good Anglo liberal, don't we? Well, hell, tell him the truth. . . . We've been hurting for a long time."[83] He justified leaving the Dem-ocratic party by saying: "Everybody was always bothered and said, 'We can't get out of the Democratic Party. Why bite the hand that feeds you?' Well, you bite it because it feeds you slop. Others say, 'Well, why don't you switch over and join the Re-publican Party?' Well, let's not even touch that one."[84] To the argument that he should work within existing parties, he re-sponded: "Why can't you begin to think very selfishly as a Chi-cano? I still haven't found a good argument from anyone as to why we should not have a Chicano party. Particularly when you are the majority. If you want to implement and see democracy in action—the will of the majority—you are not going to see it in the Democratic Party. You can only see it through a Chicano party."[85]

After rejecting existing parties, he justified forming a third party: "The third party is a very viable kind of alternative. It's a solution. For once you can sit in your own courthouse and you don't have to talk about community control because you are the community. . . . We are talking about bringing some very basic elements into the lives of mexicanos—like education and like making urban renewal work for mexicanos instead of being the new way of stealing land."[86] His new approach, then, was "to produce constituencies to elect Mexican-Americans to office who will promote the interests of Mexican-Americans only."[87]

CONCLUSION

As the Chicano leader with the most formal education, Gu-tierrez had studied theories of the organization of mass move-ments. Successfully adapting these theories to the specific needs of Mexican-Americans in his home town, he helped to found a Chicano political party, La Raza Unida, as the major vehicle to reach his political goals. When the party was firmly established, he and other Mexican-Americans successfully ran for office and demonstrated that they could use the Anglo political structure to their own advantage. Once in a position of power, Gutierrez attempted to implement the demands of Chicanos in south Texas.

Gutierrez was well prepared as an advocate. His early training in competitive speech contests and his later persuasive writings taught him how to communicate effectively with audiences of Mexican-Americans and Anglos. In his campaign in Crystal City, he frequently employed his skills as a speaker and a writer before Mexican-American audiences.

The rhetoric Gutierrez created was well suited for south Texas at the time. He sought to redefine Mexican-Americans by labeling them as Chicanos and to add solidarity in the community through such terms as Aztlan and La Raza as well as through the depiction of the Anglo as devil. He also strove to restructure the Mexican-American's reality, arguing that Chicanos had a history of dissent, were not inferior due to their color, had not lost their heritage, and possessed a significant history. The past and present problems of Chicanos, Gutierrez insisted, resulted from the inability of older Mexican-Americans to fight the Anglo and resist the oppressive efforts of the Anglo's institutions. In order to change this pattern of failure, he called for young Chicanos to unite into a separate political party, La Raza Unida.

Gutierrez rarely threatened to carry out violence. Instead he substituted the threat of destroying Anglos through political means, a threat which was more fitting for Chicano audiences and allowed them to pursue pragmatic options in their battle for their culture and rights. Such adaptation was consistent with his belief that the "Chicano movement had developed much that is indigenous to itself and learned to recast its myths to serve the revolution and define the enemy within and the enemy without.... And even more important, it has learned to recognize the friend within and the friend without."[88]

NOTES

1. F. Chris Garcia and Rudolph O. de la Garza, *The Chicano Political Experience: Three Perspectives* (North Scituate, Mass.: Duxbury Press, 1977), p. 156.

2. Ibid., p. 171.

3. Ibid.

4. Tony Castro, *Chicano Power: The Emergence of Mexican America* (New York: Saturday Review Press, 1974), p. 149. His father died when Gutierrez was a teenager, and the family did have some financial problems after his death. In a personal interview, Gutierrez told the authors how his father had been an activist in south Texas.

5. John Staples Shockley, *Chicano Revolt in a Texas Town* (Notre Dame, Ind.: University of Notre Dame Press, 1974), p. 122.

6. Calvin Trillin, "U.S. Journal: Crystal City, Texas," *New Yorker*, 17 April 1971, p. 104.

7. Trillin, p. 104.

8. Richard J. Jensen, "An Interview with Jose Angel Gutierrez," *Western Journal of Speech Communication* 44 (Summer 1980), p. 204.

9. Quoted in Shockley, p. 37. On pages 24 through 110, Shockley gives a thorough description of the 1963 election and its aftermath.

10. Jose Angel Gutierrez, *La Raza and Revolution* (San Francisco: R and E Research Associates, 1972), p. 1. This is a published version of Gutierrez's M.A. thesis at St. Mary's University in San Antonio.

11. Quoted in Castro, p. 155.

12. MAYO pamphlet quoted in Shockley, p. 114.

13. Shockley, p. 114.

14. Ibid.

15. Ibid., p. 90.

16. Ibid.

17. Jose Angel Gutierrez, "Gutierrez at the University of Texas," speech presented at the University of Texas on 13 November 1970, in Robert Tice, "Rhetoric of La Raza," unpublished manuscript, 1971, Chicano Studies Collection, Arizona State University, Tempe, Arizona, p. 13, appendix. A copy is in the possession of the authors.

18. Shockley, p. 126.

19. Jose Angel Gutierrez, "Mexicanos Need to Control Their Own Destinies," in *La Raza Unida Party in Texas* (New York: Pathfinder Press, 1971), p. 13.

20. The problems in the school centered on issues like selection of cheerleaders, racist attitudes of teachers toward Chicano students, and lack of sensitivity to the needs of Chicano students. As a skilled organizer, Gutierrez sought such issues in order to facilitate action.

21. Jose Angel Gutierrez, *The Walkout of 1969: A Diary of Events* (Crystal City, Tex.: Building Trades, 1979), p. 2. Gutierrez found that many of the male members of the Mexican-American community tried to shift responsibility by having him approach their wives on any issue dealing with schools. The women were "eager, if not anxious, to confront whomever in behalf of their children."

22. Gutierrez, *The Walkout of 1969*, p. 2.

23. Ibid., p. 3. This tactic resulted in men becoming actively involved in fighting the school board on the issues. It was an appeal to the manhood of the community.

24. Changes were made in the selection of cheerleaders and school queens, and policies were changed concerning the treatment of Chicanos in general. It was viewed as a great victory.

25. Shockley, p. 124.

26. Garcia and de la Garza, p. 164.

27. Gutierrez was reelected in 1978 but resigned in 1981 before finishing his term.

28. Ricard O. Sanchez, "Editor's Preface," in Jose Angel Gutierrez, *El Politico* (El Paso, Tex.: Mictla Publications, 1972), p. ii.

29. Jose Angel Gutierrez, *A Gringo Manual* (Crystal City, Tex.: Wintergarden Publishing House, n.d.), p. iv.

30. Ibid., p. 88.

31. Gutierrez, "Gutierrez at the University of Texas," p. 2.

32. Ibid., pp. 3–4.

33. Gutierrez, *La Raza and Revolution*, p. 1.

34. Garcia and de la Garza, p. 199.

35. Gutierrez, *La Raza and Revolution*, p. 30.

36. Jose Angel Gutierrez, "A Youth Manifesto," in *Manifesto Addressed to the President of the United States from the Youth of America*, ed. Alan Rinzler (London: Collier Books, 1970), p. 72.

37. Gutierrez, "The Chicano and Education," p. 8.

38. In "An Interview with Jose Angel Gutierrez" (p. 205), he states that in speaking to a Chicano audience "you wouldn't attack the Virgin Mary, you wouldn't attack the church." The Catholic Church has been a strong force in the Mexican-American community, and any attacks on it would immediately alienate many members of the audience.

39. Although Gutierrez used the word *brown* in an attempt to create solidarity, he preferred the word *bronce* (bronze). "Even the most Spanish Spaniards in New Mexico will love *la raza de bronce* (the bronze race). It connotes richness." See "An Interview with Jose Angel Gutierrez," p. 210.

40. Quoted in Patty Newman, *Do It Up Brown!* (San Diego: Viewpoint Books, 1971), p. 43.

41. Quoted in Castro, p. 149.

42. Ibid., p. 41.

43. Gutierrez, "Mexicanos Need to Control Their Own Destinies," pp. 10–11.

44. Gutierrez, "A Youth Manifesto," pp. 68–69.

45. Gutierrez, *El Politico*, p. 3.

46. Gutierrez, "A Youth Manifesto," p. 67.

47. Jose Angel Gutierrez, "La Raza and Revolution," in *Readings in La Raza*, ed. Matt S. Meier and Feliciano Rivera (New York: Hill and Wang, 1974), p. 235.

48. Gutierrez, *A Gringo Manual*, p. 30.

49. Ibid., p. 88.

50. Quoted in Castro, p. 157.

51. Gutierrez, "Gutierrez at the University of Texas," p. 4.

52. Gutierrez, "The Chicano and Education," p. 2.

53. Ibid., p. 3.

54. Ibid., p. 5.

55. Gutierrez, *El Politico*, p. 2.

56. Gutierrez, "Gutierrez at the University of Texas," p. 7.

57. Gutierrez, *La Raza and Revolution*, p. 52.

58. Gutierrez, "Gutierrez at the University of Texas," pp. 4–5.

59. Ibid., p. 5.

60. Gutierrez, *La Raza and Revolution*, p. 31.

61. Ibid., pp. 24–37.

62. Gutierrez, *A Gringo Manual*, pp. 5 and 9.

63. Trillin, p. 105.

64. Gutierrez, "Gutierrez at the University of Texas," p. 14.

65. Gutierrez, "The Chicano and Education," p. 26.

66. Gutierrez, "Mexicanos Need to Control Their Own Destinies," p. 11.

67. Gutierrez, "The Chicano and Education," p. 21.

68. Gutierrez, *La Raza and Revolution*, p. 66.

69. Quoted in Castro, p. 182.

70. Gutierrez, "A Youth Manifesto," p. 73.

71. Gutierrez, "Gutierrez at the University of Texas," p. 12.

72. Gutierrez, "A Youth Manifesto," p. 70.

73. Ibid.

74. Author's Interview with Jose Angel Gutierrez, Crystal City, Texas, 28 January 1980.

75. Shockley, p. 284 n. 112.

76. Shockley, p. 231. Taken from the *Congressional Record*, 15 April 1969.

77. Gutierrez, "Gutierrez at the University of Texas," p. 16.

78. Gutierrez, "Mexicanos Need to Control Their Own Destinies," p. 14.

79. Ibid., p. 12.

80. Ibid., p. 11.

81. Quoted in Martin Waldron, "New Mexican-American Party Hails Growth of Brown Power," *New York Times*, 3 September 1973, 4, p. 3.

82. Gutierrez, "Mexicanos Need to Control Their Own Destinies," p. 13.

83. Ibid.

84. Ibid., p. 12.

85. Ibid.

86. Ibid., p. 14.

87. Ibid.

88. "My Revolution," in *From the Barrio*, ed. Luis Omar Salinas and Lillian Faderman (San Francisco: Canfield Press, 1973), p. 1.

6

The Rhetorical Counter-Attack of Mexican-American Political Leaders

During the years of active Chicano protest there were five members of Congress from the Mexican-American community: Representatives Henry B. Gonzalez (D-Texas), Eligio (Kika) de la Garza (D-Texas), Edward R. Roybal (D-California), and Manuel Lujan, Jr. (R-New Mexico), and Senator Joseph M. Montoya (D-New Mexico). Adept and popular politicians, the representatives had been reelected continually while Montoya served three terms in the Senate. Yet despite their successes in politics, they drew scathing attacks from some of the militant Chicanos. This chapter will examine the rhetoric of the political leaders, illuminating central issues in the often acrimonious dialogue between the two factions.

Henry B. Gonzalez was clearly the most outspoken Establishment leader. His series of anti-militant speeches in the House of Representatives reveals sharp differences as well as areas of agreement in the respective rhetorical visions of politicians and militants. After introducing the legislators, this chapter will focus on Gonzalez's speeches, comparing them to the rhetoric of other Establishment leaders when appropriate.[1]

MEXICAN-AMERICAN POLITICAL LEADERS

Henry B. Gonzalez was born on 3 May 1916 in San Antonio, Texas, the son of Leonides and Genevieve Barbosa Gonzalez.

His parents had fled from Mexico and settled in San Antonio in 1911. Gonzalez's father was editor of a Spanish-language newspaper which "became the voice of Mexican intellectuals and politicians" who lived in San Antonio at the time.[2] Young Henry thus grew up in a home that stressed knowledge and education. He attended San Antonio Junior College, the University of Texas at Austin, and St. Mary's University School of Law. After leaving college he worked for a series of bilingual publications, served as chief probation officer for Bexar County, Texas, and taught math and citizenship classes in a veterans training program.

Gonzalez was elected to the San Antonio City Council from 1956 to 1958 where he persistently spoke against "segregation in general and specifically against segregation of public facilities."[3] In 1956 he successfully campaigned for the State Senate, attracting national attention as the first elected Mexican-American senator in Texas history.[4] In 1957 ten bills were introduced in an attempt to circumvent federal court rulings on segregation. Gonzalez and Senator Abraham Kazen of Loredo filibustered for over thirty-six hours in an attempt to defeat the bills. During the filibuster, Gonzalez eloquently addressed the subject of hate: "It may be some can chloroform their conscience. But if we fear long enough, we hate, and if we hate long enough, we fight."[5] He also offered a memorable challenge to whites: "Well, what's the difference? Mexican, Negro, what have you? The assault on the inward dignity of man, which our society protects, has been made. . . . For whom does the bell toll? You, the white man, think it tolls for the Negro. I say, the bell tolls for you. It's ringing for us all."[6] Such language gave Gonzalez a reputation as an eloquent activist.

Elected to Congress in 1961, Gonzalez consistently defined himself as a loyal liberal Democrat. In 1961 he stated: "I regard myself as an unreconstructed, fighting American liberal of the old school. . . . Live and let live, every man has his virtue, all are equal before the law."[7] He championed civil rights in the United States and closer relationships with Latin American countries. His work in Congress represented interests of "the poor, the middle-income earners, and small business people."[8]

Eligio (Kika) de la Garza was born on 22 September 1927 in Mercedes, Texas. He attended Edinburg Junior College and St.

Mary's Law School. After duty in the navy during World War II, he served in the Texas Legislature for twelve years and then was elected to Congress in 1964. Among the Mexican-American congressmen, only de la Garza supported Gonzalez during his anti-militant orations in the House of Representatives. De la Garza chaired the Committee on Agriculture.[9]

Edward R. Roybal was born in Albuquerque, New Mexico, on 10 February 1916. In 1922 he moved to California where he attended and graduated from high school, then joined the Civilian Conservation Corps, and later studied business administration at the University of California at Los Angeles and Southwestern University in Los Angeles. After army duty during World War II, he worked as a social worker and public educator with the California Tuberculosis Association and was elected to the Los Angeles City Council. He joined Congress in 1962 and chaired the Subcommittee on Treasury, Postal Service, and General Government of the Appropriations Committee; the Housing and Consumer Interests Subcommittee of the Select Committee on Aging; and the National Association of Latino Elected Officials and Congressional Hispanic Caucus.[10]

Manuel Lujan, Jr., the only Republican among the Mexican-American congressmen, was born in San Ildefonso, New Mexico, on 12 May 1928. He graduated from the College of Santa Fe and then worked in a family insurance business. Lujan was the least active orator and legislator in the group, devoting his time to solving the individual problems of his constituents. Unlike his Mexican-American colleagues, he had a reputation as a fiscal conservative. He proclaimed: "I sincerely believe that private enterprise can do a task for less money than the federal government."[11] Elected to Congress in 1968, he served on the Committees on Interior and Insular Affairs and on Science and Technology.[12]

Senator Joseph M. Montoya was born in Pena Blanca, New Mexico, on 24 September 1915. At the age of twenty-one, while a law student at Georgetown University, he began his political career by running successfully for the New Mexico House of Representatives. The youngest member of the state legislature, he soon became lieutenant governor. In 1957 he was elected to the U.S. House of Representatives and in 1964 to the Senate.

During these years he amassed considerable wealth through his business dealings, wealth which brought him criticism from young Chicanos. Montoya completed three terms and died soon after his unsuccessful campaign for reelection in 1976.[13]

These five leaders had much in common. Each was college educated, had a successful private career, and remained in Congress for many years. As middle-aged, middle-class members of the Establishment, they were apart from the average Chicano. When militants criticized them for being representatives of established privilege, however, Gonzalez led an aggressive counter-attack. His counter-charges fit into four themes: (1) the young radicals practiced reverse racism and preached hate solely on the basis of race; (2) they displayed ignoble qualities and harmed the Mexican-American community; (3) the Ford Foundation was misled into funding their cause; and (4) the young militants were unfair and personal in their attacks against him.

ATTACKING THE MILITANTS

Portraying the radicals as racists consumed with debilitating hatred, Gonzalez reported to his listeners: "I have watched with alarm as new Mexican-American militant groups have formed, not because they have formed, but because some of them . . . have fallen into the spell of reverse racism."[14] These young people, admittedly victims of racism in their own lives, "have adopted the same poisons, the same attitudes, the same tactics of those who have so long offended them."[15] This reverse racism, continued Gonzalez, led "self-appointed leaders" into making "facile judgements of large classes of people, using the same sort of distorted logic, deceitful tongues, and hateful words of racists."[16] He contended that one could not characterize any ethnic group as all good or all bad; yet the activists were portraying all Anglos as bad and all Chicanos as good. Gonzalez concluded that such black-and-white reasoning made the young Chicanos no better than white supremacists. In agreement with Gonzalez, de la Garza claimed that while past injustices could not be denied, the new militants were "turning it around to the point where they do not want justice, but they want to bring about injustice upon those who they feel brought it to them in the past. . . . This is just racism in reverse and it is something that we cannot condone."[17]

Reverse racism led some activists to view themselves as ultimate judges, Gonzalez charged, for "to these new racists, the key to being good or evil depends on whether they personally approve of you or not."[18] This new racism "demands an allegiance to race above all else."[19] While some radicals required total loyalty from all members of the Mexican-American community, they also proclaimed the right to expel anyone from the community who did not accept their views. "Only one thing counts to them," Gonzalez asserted, "loyalty to la raza above all else, and MAYO (Mexican-American Youth Organization) next. Of course they reserve the right to judge who is loyal and who is not."[20]

Gonzalez blamed such radicals for losing sight of the real goal of any minority group: "These people do not want justice," he declared, "They do not want equality—they want to get even—not to get equal."[21] Ironically, this misguided idealism promoted the same ugly racism the radicals were attempting to overcome. Thus, the radicals were motivated by ignoble desires for power to judge others and for satisfaction through revenge.

In his outline of the consequences of racial hatred, Gonzalez warned that you "cannot fan the flames of emotion, or turn on the streams of bigotry one moment and expect them to disappear the next."[22] Although racism was evil and must be fought at every turn, the actions of these young people would only escalate existing bad feeling: "an injustice to one side may lead to another injustice on the other."[23]

Gonzalez agreed with the young leaders that anger was justified by the great suffering of Mexican-Americans for many years, but he pointed out that anger alone would not solve anything: "It is easy to be angry, but it is hard to have that moral indignation that alone reveals the depth of injustice and lights the corridor of truth."[24] The anger set off by militants could cause problems that would take generations to solve. Gonzalez also agreed with many of the goals of the militants, but he rejected their means:

I cannot accept the belief that racism in reverse is the answer for racism and discrimination; I cannot accept the belief that simple, blind, and stupid hatred is an adequate response to simple, blind, and stupid hatred; I cannot accept the belief that playing at revolution produces anything beyond an excited imagination; and I cannot accept the belief that imitation leadership is a substitute for the real thing. . . . There are those who believe that the best answer for hate is hate in reverse, and that the best leadership is that which is loudest and most arrogant; but my observation is that arrogance is no cure for emptiness.[25]

Montoya also saw problems with the militants' actions. He, too, worried that "the last thing the Spanish-speaking need is agitation, rabble-rousing or creation of false hopes."[26] Although he was specifically referring to Tijerina, Montoya's comments could be applied to all Chicano militants.

After defining his Chicano adversaries as racists in reverse, Gonzalez unleashed a rhetorical barrage against the Ford Foundation.[27] The Ford grant which established the Southwest Council of La Raza and provided it $630,000 to create a national organization "rested on a false assumption; namely, that such a disparate group could, any more than our black brothers or our white 'Anglo' brothers, be brought under one large tent."[28] Rather than creating the desired unity, the grant "has so far created disunity; and where it aimed to coordinate it has only further unloosed the conflicting aims and desires of various groups and individuals."[29]

Gonzalez accused the Ford Foundation of "simply financing the ambitions of some men who are greedy and some who are ruthless and a few who are plainly irresponsible."[30] These individuals, mostly from the Mexican-American Youth Organization (MAYO), used foundation money to form unnecessary organizations and stock them with inept leaders. The rapid growth of militant leadership made it virtually impossible even to discover where the money was being spent. Those who spent Ford money, concluded Gonzalez, strove primarily to create jobs for friends.

Turning to specific individuals and organizations covered by the grant, Gonzalez scrutinized the leader of MAYO, Jose Angel Gutierrez, who was receiving Ford Foundation money as a legal investigator: "The interesting aspect of the job is that Gutierrez is not a lawyer. . . . His job leaves him ample time to travel and speak on behalf of MAYO, so that one wonders whether he investigates as much as he instigates."[31] Why give money to an organization headed by a "25–year-old person who never had the experience of even holding a regular job,"[32] asked Gonzalez. Moreover, Gutierrez preached hate in his speeches and espoused ideals of the Cuban Revolution. "Jose Angel Gutierrez may think himself something of a hero," reasoned Gonzalez, "but he is ... only a benighted soul if he believes that in the espousal of hatred he will find love. He is simply deluded if he believes that the wearing of fatigues and a beard makes his followers revolutionaries, or that the genius of revolution is in slogans."[33] Gonzalez added regretfully that these young men had taken trips to Cuba, received money from Cuba, and were trying to fashion a miniature Cuba in southern Texas. Unnamed outsiders, averred Gonzalez, "want to use the militants for their own purposes."[34]

On several occasions Gonzalez criticized an organization set up under the grant to work with delinquents, La Universidad of the Barrios (University of the Neighborhoods). He noted that the university had a college junior for a dean, lacked any curricula or classes, and had become a haven for tough characters and drinking bouts. Once, he noted, a murder was committed on the premises.[35] Gonzalez reviewed the situation:

Neighbors told me that they were terrified of the young men who hung around there, that their children had been threatened and that they were afraid to call the police. After the murder, the "dean" of this "university" said that he could not be there all the time and was not responsible for what happened while he was away. This might be true, but the general fear of the neighbors indicates that the "university" is not under reliable guidance at any time.[36]

De la Garza also assailed the militants for their actions and Communist ties. He spoke about an incident in Kingsville, Texas:

If you read and study the countries that have succumbed to communism ... you will find that the Communists come to the young people and the very youngest in the group in Kingsville were from a junior high school, and they are instilling in them the insidious hate against anything and anyone they do not understand. ... They are driving them away from their church, from their religion . . . and now they cloak some of their actions through the use of misguided or renegade members of the cloth, thus trying to give sanctity to the hatred they preach.[37]

Montoya did not call his opponents Communists, but he did refer to Tijerina as an "outsider" who "sparked violence and set back racial relations . . . an enemy of the United States and a damned liar."[38] Among his labels for Tijerina were "discredited charlatan, monster, racist, and creature of darkness."[39] Montoya excoriated the ties between Tijerina and other minority groups: "Spanish-Americans . . . will make no alliances with black nationalists who hate America. We do not lie down in the gutter with Ron Karenga, Stokely Carmichael, and Rap Brown—who seek to put another wound in America's body."[40]

Gonzalez's primary complaint was that the militants were ineffective imitators who played at revolution. He elaborated:

We have those who cry "brown power" only because they have heard "black power" and we have those who yell "oink" or "pig" at police, only because they have heard others use the term. We have those who wear beards and berets, not because they attach any meaning to it, but because they have seen it done elsewhere. But neither fervor nor fashion alone will bring justice. Those who cry for justice, but hold it in contempt cannot win it for themselves or for anyone else. Those who prize power for its own sake will never be able to use it for any benefit but their own; and those who can only follow the fashions of protest will never understand what true protest is.[41]

The one Chicano leader acceptable to the political spokesmen was Cesar Chavez, easily the most moderate of the new militants. This acceptance was perhaps best expressed by Montoya:

The most notable success achieved by Spanish-speaking Americans has been through the religious-oriented nonviolent Union of Farmworkers of Cesar Chavez. His bitter drawn-out struggle inches along in the face of staggering obstacles. Younger Chicanos admire him but also note the barriers consistently thrown in his path. Most do not feel they should have to battle so long for elementary progress on a road traveled successfully long ago by so many others."[42]

Roybal echoed Montoya's sentiment, depicting the farm workers' historical lack of power and organization and maintaining
that the movement's recent successes "depended very much on
its plea to the American public for basic justice and fair play.
. . . For the most part Americans have responded, they have
championed the farmworkers' cry for justice and fair wages."[43]

Gonzalez did not ignore accusations against himself. Militants
had tried to divert attention from their own inefficiency by opposing him and his proposals, shifting attention from the real
problem: the defeat of "poverty, hopelessness, and despair" in
the Mexican-American community.[44] Labeling such charges
against him as unfair, he answered: "I do not represent any
conglomerate group. . . . Some of these young men say 'I speak
for five million people.' Do they? I wonder."[45] He compared
himself to his antagonists in this manner: "I believe that a just
and decent cause can be undermined by those who believe there
is no decency, and who demand for themselves what they would
deny others. I have stood against racists before, and I will gladly
do it again; and I have stood against blind passion before and I
will gladly do it again."[46]

Recalling similar antagonism, Gonzalez recounted being called
a Communist, a Fabian Socialist, a nigger-lover, and "denigrated
as a wrecker of stability and destroyer of harmony" by "right-
wing extremists."[47] Although the current charges were unusual,
his course of action would not change:

I now find myself assaulted from the left as well as from the right. Yet
I do not hesitate to say now, as before, that evil is evil, that it is just
as wrong for a member of an ethnic minority to succumb to hate and
fear as it is for anyone else to do so. A racist is no good either to himself
or to his fellow men, be he black, white, brown, red, or yellow. I believe
in decency, and I denounce indecency; and I serve public notice that
my policy will not change.[48]

Gonzalez cited his own career to illustrate "that walls of prejudice can crumble. . . . You will be heard from when you have
something to offer."[49] Proof that his efforts had been correct
came from the support and behavior of many Americans. He
stated:

My faith has been affirmed time and again in the basic decency and integrity of the vast and overwhelming majority of the people in this land. I have seen it proved all over the country that there is far more decency than indecency, far more tolerance than intolerance, and far more honor than dishonor. That has made it worthwhile; that has removed the sting from the barbs of haters both professional and amateur alike; and that has enabled me to say truthfully that the haters are a small and contemptible minority.[50]

PROPOSALS FOR CHANGE

The established political leaders proposed solutions to problems facing Mexican-Americans. Unlike the militants who chose to work outside the system, these political leaders sought to accomplish their proposals by being bargainers committed to working within the system. These leaders were convinced that "only by participating in mainstream politics could Chicanos derive any benefits from the dominant society."[51] Rather than forming their own parties in the manner of Gutierrez, Gonzales, and Tijerina, these politicians labored in the Democratic and Republican parties and thereby showed a deep faith in the American political process—a faith abandoned by the activists.

Gonzalez revealed the basis of his faith:

This is no land of cynics, and it is no land of demagogues; it is a land wherein I believe reason can prevail; if it cannot succeed here it can succeed nowhere. . . . I believe that however slowly and painfully we may be doing it, our country is overcoming the forces of racism. I believe that the impetus of racism is spent, or very nearly so, and that it is possible that justice in this land can be achieved within legitimate means.[52]

He then delineated his version of justice:

I mean decent work at decent wages for all who want to work; decent support for those who cannot support themselves; full and equal opportunity in employment, in education, in schools; I mean by justice the full, fair, and impartial protection of the law for every man; I mean by justice decent homes, adequate streets and public services; and I mean by justice no man being asked to do more than his fair share, but none expected to do less. In short, I seek a justice that amounts to full, free, and equal opportunity for all; I believe in a justice that does not tolerate evil or evil doing; and I believe in a justice that is for all the people all the time.[53]

This fairness could be achieved by individuals who knew what they wanted and had a plan to achieve it, according to Gonzalez, and not "by vague and empty gestures, or by high slogans uttered by orators who are present today and gone tomorrow."[54]

Each political leader believed that social progress for Mexican-Americans could come only through steady change over a long period. Perceiving progress in his lifetime, Gonzalez told the radicals: "Social progress at last is coming at a satisfactory rate; do not jeopardize that by extremism."[55] Roybal also claimed that progress was occurring, and he pictured Mexican-Americans as "law-abiding Americans who have not resorted to riot and civil disobedience and need just a little help to enable them to lift themselves from their status of poverty and neglect."[56] Verbalizing his vision of progress, Montoya depicted Mexican-Americans in this manner: "Their eyes look up or forward, rather than down. Their hats remain on their heads, instead of being in their hands. Truly a new age is upon us."[57]

These Congressmen were committed to government programs as the best vehicle for change. "The Government," directed Gonzalez, "must now take steps to see that the new dreams of the Spanish-surnamed American population are turned into realities."[58] Citing as evidence of successful government programs the Job Corps, the Neighborhood Youth Corps, and VISTA, he pictured an optimistic future: "Most of all, there is a reviving feeling among the poor, and among the Spanish-surnamed, that it really is possible to get better. . . . If the government can capitalize on those feelings there can be progress."[59] Roybal added: "Throughout the area they are now participating in new, vital programs that have brought so much new awareness to many of them."[60] The next step, Gonzalez continued, was for the government to match its inspirational words with concrete actions:

Having provided the sustenance of hope and the fires of ambition, the Government must now take steps. . . . No man's hunger is satisfied if he is only shown a menu: food alone will suffice. The vigor and leadership that have so far been offered must be continued, even redoubled.[61]

If government did not satisfy the new expectations of Mexican-Americans, serious problems would occur. "The Spanish-speaking citizens of our Southwest are astir," said Montoya, "and we must take heed of those stirrings. Not to do so would be the height of folly and the depth of ignorance of legitimate aspirations."[62] "I see ominous portents of things to come," he confessed, "a small but growing group in our Spanish-speaking community is beginning to despair of making real progress. It feels only deliberately fostered turbulence will awaken our power structure and Nation to their needs. I reject such an approach entirely, yet certainly understand both the motivation, frustration behind it."[63] His implication was clear: the country must choose between the militants or the established leaders; whatever the choice, the lives of Mexican-Americans must change soon. One practice that had to be changed immediately was that fostered by the media: "Consider the image scores of millions of Americans presently entertain regarding Spanish-speaking Americans. That mental picture is a totally degrading stereotype. . . . A sleepy, lazy, dirty Mexican in a sombrero dozing under a cactus. A greasy-looking, overweight, bandit type with bandoleers slung across his body, galloping off to stir a tinpot revolution. An image of a person lacking ambition, honesty, elementary habits of hygiene and self-respect."[64] Congressman Roybal concurred: "There are still repeated instances where Mexicans are portrayed in a degrading and ridiculing manner. It is my hope that we can stop perpetuating and selling to the public this type of immature and racist humor which not only demeans a culturally rich people but all Americans."[65]

Establishment leaders also objected to the treatment of Mexican-Americans by the legal system. They argued that a double standard treated Anglos differently from Mexican-Americans. Montoya itemized the abuses: excessive police violence, unfair use of arrest power, bail denials, underrepresentation on juries, and lack of interpreters to clarify their rights. Several of the leaders mentioned discriminatory actions by J. Edgar Hoover and Judge Gerald S. Chargin.[66] These concerns paralleled the complaints of Chicano leaders, with the primary difference being the means advocated to remedy the injustices.

Mexican-Americans also endured unjustified hardships in the

military. Noting the "disproportionate numbers" drafted into the armed forces, the political leaders marshalled statistics on the casualties in Vietnam. For example, Montoya found that "Defense Department figures show 44.6 percent of all New Mexico fighting men killed in Vietnam between 1961 and 1967 were Spanish-surnamed. Yet, about 30 percent of the population of New Mexico is Hispano-surnamed."[67]

The willingness of Mexican-Americans to fight for their country brought them few rewards upon leaving the military. Montoya elaborated: "They were adequate for utilization as cannon fodder in Asia, but are rarely considered good enough to qualify for equal treatment back home."[68] These young veterans would be forced into dissent and even violence, he forecast, if their needs were not met. The threat to the Establishment was clear: either reforms were forthcoming or society faced violence from its Hispanic veterans.

The road to prevent such dissent and violence led to increased political power within the community. "Politically, we are the most underrepresented group in the country, except for Indians," Montoya reported.[69] Mexican-Americans must make clear that they would no longer be dismissed politically: "For years we have been taken for granted by both political parties. We have heard more promises than a drunkard's wife. Almost all have been broken."[70] To remedy the problem, Mexican-Americans must unify into a potent political force to gain their rights. Congressman Roybal expressed the need for cultural solidarity: "the search for unity is more than a search for symbolic cultural solidarity. It is more than a dream—more than mere defense against continuing inequities committed against the Spanish-speaking people. It is the strong human desire for self preservation, a desire that compels us to seek a united strategy to overcome the many problems which weigh most heavily on us."[71] Thus, the political leaders chose not to reject the traditional parties as the young activists did, but to build sufficient power to influence the traditional parties.

Unity required a galvanizing term. Gonzalez outlined this need: "There is not even a generally accepted name for this minority group.... Mexican, Mexicanos, Latins, Latinos, Latin Americans, and Hispanic Americans; not one of these labels is accepted." Discarding hyphenated terms like Mexican-American as too narrow, he proposed the label "Americans of Spanish surname." "I prefer to think of the group as Americans of Spanish surname because," he said,

after all, they are Americans and they all have Spanish surnames. Any other label would be inadequate because this group has such diverse origins. Some were born here and some have immigrated only recently. Some come from families that have lived in the Southwest for more than 200 years and are of Spanish descent. Others have origins in Mexico of parentage ranging from Indian tribes to English gentry. There is no term, perhaps even one so tentlike as Spanish-surnamed American, that adequately describes a group so conglomerate as this."[72]

A case was also made for Mexican-American, Hispanic, or Spanish-speaking as an inclusive term, with no one label being acceptable to all leaders. Although the term *Chicano* was rejected, the power of that word was acknowledged: "In their [the militants'] mouths it becomes a term of pride. . . . Such people look at our world through new eyes. . . . All they seek is a chance. Yet, it is just that which America continues to deny them."[73]

Along with a new term of identification must come a new national organization which would center its initial effort on securing employment for Mexican-Americans. To Congressman Roybal this national organization could "balance our display of strength with mutual respect for each other, regardless of our past disagreements, our differences in ideology, status or party affiliation."[74] This organization had to pressure the federal government to provide jobs because, as Lujan stated succinctly: "If there is a job, most other problems will fall into place."[75] Roybal coined the phrase "occupational caste system," indicting the federal government for being one of the worst offenders in denying jobs to Mexican-Americans.[76] He promised to oppose funding for any federal agency that denied job opportunities to Mexican-Americans. Gonzalez, too, was particularly concerned with unemployment and the waste of human talent. "There is no machine," he told listeners, "to explain what happens to a man when he loses hope, or when he abandons the idea that tomorrow may bring better things. Nor is there any way of reckoning the tragic cost incurred by the waste of human talents that have never been able to contribute their full value to society."[77] The human waste was illustrated by employment figures: "In a country where the rate of unemployment is below 4 percent, this minority experiences unemployment of 8 percent; in many places the figure is twice that high. . . . Many who are lucky enough to have jobs have no hope of advancing, because the Spanish-surnamed minority is, in general, undereducated and without the skills necessary for finding a good job or advancing."[78] The poverty caused by underemployment led to illnesses and illiteracy.

When Gonzalez maintained that the federal government must help these "millions of willing and able people to realize their full potential," he made clear that his was a deserving minority with a rich culture.[79] As he reminded listeners:

Americans of Spanish surname have furnished the muscles that turned much of the Southwest from arid desert into miraculously productive farmland, who laid the rails and plucked the cotton, who dug the ditches and laid the foundations of our cities, and who have willingly laid down their lives to defend it all, now know that the great American dream, so long denied, can be theirs.[80]

These contributions flowed naturally from the diverse Mexican-American heritage. He explained:

A culture is too precious to destroy . . . it must be permitted to make its own contributions to society, especially one like ours. For Americans are many things and that is the secret of our strength. It would be a mistake to think that the diversity which the Spanish-surnamed people offer is anything other than a potential gift to our already rich heritage.[81]

Montoya observed that the government should encourage a positive image of Mexican-American heritage: "It can create courses on our history and culture with little difficulty, if motivation is there. Today, we are supplying just that. Let's have action in this area now."[82]

To preserve the culture, Spanish must be taught in the schools: "A language is more than a way of communicating." Gonzalez instructed, "it is a link to the whole culture, and abandoning your mother tongue is not unlike losing a part of your soul."[83] Montoya agreed: "We must take advantage of the language pluralism that exists in the Southwest. But it must be constructive pluralism. Comprehensive bilingual education programs . . . are one way we can give to all the best of both worlds in terms of language, culture, and cooperation in daily life."[84] The failures in the school systems were obvious, for as Roybal stated: "The median years of school completed for Spanish-speaking children in the Southwest is 7.1 years whereas for the Anglo child in the Southwest, it is 12.1 years, and for the non-white child it is 9 years of school completed."[85] The twin themes of educational failure and the need for bilingual education have been continually articulated by all the political leaders.

CONCLUSION

The arguments of these Establishment political figures publicized the need for changes in the Mexican-American community. They sought improved media images for Mexican-Americans, fairer treatment in the legal system and military, solidarity in the community through a common term of self-identification and an umbrella national organization, acceptance of their culture and language, and improvement in their daily lives, particularly through better jobs and education. The politicians reasoned that such changes could occur only slowly by working within the Establishment, but they employed veiled threats that violence could occur if change did not come soon.

Although agreeing that such changes must occur, the militants proposed to reject the Establishment and create alternative political parties and organizations. The militants, in contrast to the moderates, wanted to separate themselves from society rather than to work within it. In rejecting the Establishment, the Chicano leaders also had to reject the traditional leaders. Garcia and de la Garza detail this rejection:

There are generally bad feelings attached to the whole notion of leadership in the Chicano community because in the past leadership has often been equated with selling out to the Anglo power structure or accommodating oneself to it. The price for leadership has too often been leaving behind one's Chicanoism or cultural characteristics and operating in the mode of the Anglo. Thus it is hard to convince the Chicano people that under altered political or socioeconomic circumstances there could emerge key persons who could retain their ties to the Chicano way of life and the Chicano people.[86]

Not surprisingly, no single political spokesman was accepted as a leader by the Chicano community: "To many, they are at best misguided, at worst *vendidos*. . . . None of these men can rally the entire Chicano community to their support."[87]

The failure of any elected leader to represent a large segment of the Mexican-Americans underscored the problems of developing an effective national organization for any ethnic group whose members traditionally depended on local political *jefes* or leaders. Moreover, the people's reverence for spoken words encouraged vivid rhetorical visions of past, present, and future which contrasted in important ways with the visions of leaders of other constituencies in the diverse group. Thus, while the moderate orators urged unity and expanded the almost universally accepted case among Mexican-Americans of the need for changes and the admiration of their culture, their words brought them no national followings and even separated them from more militant leaders.

NOTES

1. There were six speeches given on 3, 15, 16, 22, 28, and 29 April 1969.

2. Eugene Rodriguez, Jr., *Henry B. Gonzalez: A Political Profile* (New York: Arno Press, 1976), p. 34. Gonzalez's father operated a profitable silver mine in the state of Durango. After Francisco Madero's successful revolution in 1910, local insurgents arrested Gonzalez, threatened to kill him, and then released him after taking most of his possessions. Further information may be found in Clarke Newlon, *Famous Mexican-Americans* (New York: Dodd, Mead, and Co., 1972) and Richard J. Jensen and John C. Hammerback, "An Establishment View of the Chicano Movement: Henry B. Gonzalez," *Texas Speech Communication Journal* 7 (1982), pp. 27–36.

3. Rodriguez, p. 71. Newlon (p. 77) states that Gonzalez was ejected from a public park after being elected to the city council. That incident led him to introduce the laws desegregating all facilities.

4. Rodriguez, p. 77. Antonio Navarro, a native Texan of Spanish-Italian descent, was appointed state senator in 1846 and served one term.

5. "For Whom the Bell Tolls," *Time*, 13 May 1957, p. 27.

6. Ibid., p. 27. Also see Hart Stilwell, "Texas Rebel with a Cause," *Coronet*, August 1958, p. 46. The fact that these two quotes were picked out of a lengthy filibuster indicates the controversial nature of each.

7. Ronnie Dugger, "Lyndon Johnson's Successor," *New Republic*, 13 February 1961, p. 8.

8. Rodriguez, p. 164.

9. *1981 Congressional Directory* (Washington, D.C.: U.S. Government Printing Office, 1981), p. 171.

10. Ibid., p. 20.

11. Sven Erik Holmes, *Manuel Lujan, Jr.: Republican Representative from New Mexico* (Washington, D.C.: Grossman Publishers, 1972), p. 4.

12. *1981 Congressional Directory*, p. 112.

13. John Littlewood and Frederick Aten, *Joseph M. Montoya: Democratic Senator from New Mexico* (Washington, D.C.: Grossman Publishers, 1972), p. 3.

14. "Race Hate," *Congressional Record*, 3 April 1969, p. 8590.

15. "Cause for Concern," *Congressional Record*, 23 April 1969, p. 9058.

16. Ibid.

17. Eligio de la Garza, "Reverse Racism," *Congressional Record*, 28 April 1969, p. 10525.

18. "Cause for Concern," p. 9058.

19. Ibid.

20. De la Garza, "Reverse Racism," p. 10527.

21. Ibid., p. 10525.

22. "Race Hate," p. 8590.

23. De la Garza, "Reverse Racism," p. 10526.

24. "The Hate Issue," *Congressional Record*, 22 April 1969, p. 9952.

25. Ibid.

26. Quoted in Patricia Bell Blawis, *Tijerina and the Land Grants* (New York: International Publishers, 1971), pp. 99–100.

27. "Foundation Responsibility," *Congressional Record*, 16 April 1959, pp. 9308–9309.

28. "The Hate Issue," p. 9953.

29. Ibid.

30. "Foundation Responsibility," p. 9309.

31. "Foundation Responsibility II," *Congressional Record*, 29 April 1969, p. 10779.

32. De la Garza, "Reverse Racism," p. 10525.

33. "Race Hate," p. 8590.

34. "The Hate Issue," pp. 9952–9953.

35. "Foundation Responsibility," p. 9309.

36. "The Hate Issue," p. 9953.

37. De la Garza, "Reverse Racism," p. 10524.

38. Quoted in Blawis, pp. 99–100.

39. Ibid., pp. 100–101.

40. Ibid., p. 100.

41. "The Hate Issue," p. 9953.

42. Joseph M. Montoya, "Woe Unto Those Who Have Ears But Do Not Hear," in *La Causa Politica*, ed. F. Chris Garcia (Notre Dame, Ind.: University of Notre Dame Press, 1974), p. 5.

43. Edward R. Roybal, "The Government Denies Justice to the Farmworkers," *Congressional Record*, 30 March 1972, p. 11323.

44. "Cause for Concern," p. 9058.

45. Quoted in Newlon, p. 87.

46. "The Hate Issue," p. 9953.

47. "Race Hate," p. 8590.

48. Ibid.

49. Quoted in Rodriguez, p. 109.

50. "Race Hate," p. 8590.

51. F. Chris Garcia and Rudolph O. de la Garza, *The Chicano Political Experience: Three Perspectives* (North Scituate, Mass.: Duxbury Press, 1977), p. 156.

52. "Reverse Racism," p. 10527.

53. "The Hate Issue," p. 9952.

54. Ibid.

55. Quoted in "Texas 'Sleeping Giant'—Really Awake This Time?" *Texas Observer*, 11 April 1969, p. 3.

56. Edward R. Roybal, Debate on "Cabinet Committee on Opportunities for Spanish-Speaking People," *Congressional Record—House*, 16 December 1969, p. 39395.

57. Joseph M. Montoya, " 'The Silent People' No Longer," *Congressional Record—Senate*, 17 November 1967, p. 33024.

58. Henry B. Gonzalez, "The Mexican-American: An Awakening Giant," *Employment Service Reviews*, July 1967, p. 12.

59. Gonzalez, p. 12.

60. Ibid.

61. Ibid.

62. Joseph M. Montoya, "Elementary and Secondary Education Amendments Act of 1967," *Congressional Record—Senate*, 5 December 1967, p. 35053.

63. Montoya, "Woe Unto Those," p. 6.

64. Ibid.

65. Edward R. Roybal, "Modern Advertising Practices," *Congressional Record*, 23 February 1972, p. 5311.

66. These same incidents were often discussed by Chicano leaders.

67. Montoya, "Woe Unto Those," p. 4.

68. Ibid.

69. Joseph M. Montoya, "National Spanish Speaking Coalition Conference," *Congressional Record*, 29 October 1971, p. 38356.

70. Ibid.

71. Ibid.

72. Edward R. Roybal, "A Unique Gathering in the Name of Unity," *Congressional Record—Senate*, 2 November 1971, p. 38755.

73. Henry B. Gonzalez, "Hope and Promise: Americans of Spanish Surname," *American Federationist*, July 1967, p. 14.

74. Montoya, "Woe Unto Those," p. 4.

75. Montoya, "National Spanish Speaking Coalition Conference," p. 38357.

76. Montoya, "Woe Unto Those," pp. 7–8; Lujan quoted in Holmes, p. 4.

77. Edward R. Roybal, "Political Awareness Among Mexican-American People," *Congressional Record*, 23 September 1971, p. 33198.

78. Gonzalez, "Hope and Promise," p. 14.

79. Ibid., p. 13.

80. Gonzalez, "The Mexican-American," p. 13.

81. Gonzalez, "Hope and Promise," pp. 15–16.

82. Montoya, "National Spanish Speaking Coalition Conference," p. 38355.

83. Henry B. Gonzalez, "Education for the Spanish Speaking: The Role of the Federal Government," *National Elementary Principal*, November 1970, pp. 119–120.

84. Montoya, "Elementary and Secondary Education Amendment Act of 1967," pp. 35–53.

85. Debate on "Elementary and Secondary Amendments of 1969," *Congressional Record—House*, 22 April 1969, p. 9930.

86. Garcia and de la Garza, p. 153.

87. Ibid., pp. 156–157.

Ondas y Rollos (Wavelengths and Raps): The Ideology of Contemporary Chicano Rhetoric

Chicano ideology is the study of the marketplace of ideas. There is a constant search among Chicanos for those words and phrases that capture the spirit, emotion, and vision of the community in its collective consciousness. Ideas are constantly heard in the Chicano community. Some ideas last for days or months, others last for years, and many others lie dormant or are totally ignored. The ideology of a movement is carried through messages to its audiences. These messages are in the hearts and minds of the audience. Ideas wait to be articulated in order to find an echo and be crystallized. Chicano ideology is not necessarily the search for new ideas. Rather it is the dance through the years of some of the same thoughts and ethnic symbols stated in different ways by different speakers and writers.

FOUNDATIONS OF CHICANO ETHNIC SYMBOLS

Chicano ideology since the late 1960s is best understood in the context of the historical reality of this period; its principal spokesmen and spokeswomen; the Chicano community's response; and the response of white, English-speaking America. Chicano rhetoric must be traced into the past, however, to appreciate and understand the contemporary thrust of its ideas and the use of ethnic symbols. The contemporary messages, often stated as demands, of the leadership of the Chicano community can be linked directly to the continuing struggle of these men and women since 1836.

The history of Chicano ideas stems from two sources: a European, Hispanic, intellectual root and an indigenous American one. Chicanos are at once the siblings of indigenous peoples and Spanish conquistadores. Chicanos are a mestizo people, La Raza. A literal English translation of La Raza would be "the Race." In Spanish, however, a conceptual expansion of the term means the birth of a new civilization. La Raza is the confluence of civilizations, a meeting of East and West, North and South in the Americas. La Raza is the family name of all mestizos, the children of European Spanish fathers and indigenous American mothers.

An example of this confluence of civilization is the celebration of the 12th of October, El Dia de la Raza. The Spanish-speaking world in the Americas celebrates this day as the birth of the mestizo peoples. The visit of the first Hispanic, Cristobal Colon, to the Americas marks the beginning of intermarriage between natives and foreigners. El Dia de la Raza has no religious, racist, or nationalist overtones. It is a day of ethnic celebration for all members of the Spanish-language family who reside throughout this hemisphere.

On the next day, 13 October, however, Chicanos revert to facing questions about their ethnicity: What are you? Are you Chicano? Mexicano? Latino? Hispanic? American? Individuals outside the Chicano community seek to classify the entire Spanish-speaking family in this hemisphere on the generic basis of a common language. Currently, the term in vogue is Hispanic. This term, however, encompasses only the white, European (Spain), Castilian (Spanish-language) heritage, and ignores and erases the indigenous and subsequent African heritage in the Americas. As members of the mestizo family of siblings, black, Spanish-speaking Cubans or Miskitos from Nicaragua are not different from white Costa Ricans, blue-eyed New Mexicans, or Indian Peruvians. The Spanish-speaking family comprises the same peoples who struggled with impositions of foreign governments in the past. Presently, these peoples struggle against impositions by local governments in the Americas. They respond to the legal formalisms of borders, immigration policy, and national origins in an attempt to define their ethnicity and culture.

Chicanos accept a living contradiction. When speaking in Spanish, they know who and what they are; when speaking in English, however, they have an identity problem, not knowing the who, what, or where of their people. To Chicanos, the English language personifies race and class, while the Spanish language represents culture and ethnicity.

Few Chicano scholars have attempted a study of the modern state and its role in shaping ethnicity, race, and class. Claudio Veliz, a professor of sociology in Australia, argues that the architecture for the modern state, and possibly the first theory of the state, can be traced to Castile in Spain during the sixteenth century.[1] What began as a commercial trading venture to the New World ended in conquest of the indigenous peoples of the Americas. The state that developed in Mexico deliberately continued to wage war on native peoples in order to eradicate the local cultures. Again in 1860, Maximilliano, the French usurper of the Mexican government, continued the cultural genocide of all Mexican people as a state program. Today, the Mexican process of acculturation in Mexico is another term for the state strategy of Europeanizing the indigenous American of Mexico. Indeed, it is rare to find Mexican national governmental leaders whose features and other phenotypical characteristics reflect those of indigenous people, save Benito Juarez and, more recently, Gustavo Diaz Ordaz. Chicanos, as descendants of Mexicans, have inherited the Mexican contradiction of eulogizing a "Mexican" culture that is "Europeanized" and maintaining their native ethnicity.

Among students of ethnicity there are two major schools of thought: the primordialists and the instrumentalists. Primordialists, such as Clifford Geertz, believe that certain characteristics of a people are "givens" that cannot easily be changed by the person or others; consequently, groups clash with one another over those cultural "givens."[2] Each group strives to establish the dominance of their "givens" over those of others. Instrumentalists, on the other hand, believe that the stuff of ethnicity is a pool of cultural symbols.[3] These cultural symbols are religion, language, national origin, race, and heritage. The symbols are subject to the political manipulation of ethnic leaders. The instrumentalists believe that a group of people move on a path toward a sense of community. The ethnic leaders of the group manipulate their shared symbols with words that translate features of their culture into mass action. This partial move to community is accomplished by leaders articulating cultural symbols that produce cohesion within the group. The community of fellow ethnics then can continue in the pursuit of a larger community, a nation. Nationalism leads to physical separation from the main body politic (state) or can remain a troublesome numerical minority within a state (Quebec or possibly Chicanos in years to come).

Mario Barrera is the first Chicano scholar to analyze the role of the state in developing racial inequality.[4] Barrera outlines the various views of the role of the state. He examines Max Weber's classic formulation that the state is an institution that reserves for itself a monopoly of the legitimate use of force, and explores the pluralist theory of the state and C. Wright Mills's idea of the power elite. The divergent views of the neo-Marxists are presented, as is the Marxist view that the state is the instrument utilized by one class for the domination of another. In regard to Chicanos, Barrera argues that the United States of America used violence to tear the Southwest from Mexican control. A further use of violence was in the formal and informal expropriation of land from the Mexicans that remained in the borderlands. In the quest for the regulation of labor, the modern U.S. state established a colonial labor system that consisted of a segmented labor force along ethnic and racial lines. Each segment of the labor force was systematically maintained in a subordinate position by the state.

Another Chicano scholar, Alberto Camarillo, adds to Barrera's discussion of the state.[5] He presents an excellent descriptive narrative of the transformation from Mexican pueblos to Chicano barrios. In so doing, he details the legal and extra-legal formalisms that rendered destitute the Mexicanos in the area of Santa Barbara, specifically, and southern California, in general, from 1848 to 1930.

These authors and this writer believe that the original contradictions of culture and ethnicity were compounded by an American economic design that created for Chicanos a system that stressed race and class for the explicit purpose of subordination and domination. Since the conquest, Chicanos have searched for answers to their contradictions. The search has led to various ethnic leaders who manipulate the ethnic symbols of the Chicano culture. In this stock of symbols from such sources as language, religion, race, heritage, and national origin, Chicano rhetors have found the tools to define their Chicano reality. Chicanos have a markedly different historical reality than blacks and other ethnic minority groups. Unike blacks, Chicanos were not brought to the United States of America; rather, the U.S. border came to them deep into what was once Mexico. Chicanos became a hostage people with the Treaty of Guadalupe Hidalgo in 1848. Chicanos and Mexicans from Mexico have not respected the border as a barrier that separates us from them. Other ethnic groups, mostly European and now Asian and Cuban, have chosen to come to the United States. Many other immigrant groups have strong political, economic, and religious interests within the United States to assist them in relocation, resettlement, and integration. In contrast, Mexicans and now Central Americans have always been hunted by U.S. authorities as illegal aliens.

Historically, Chicanos residing primarily in the Southwest have shared a border with Mexico of more than 2,000 miles. The border neither excludes nor separates the Mexican culture. Daily through radio transmissions, schools, business, television, newspapers, cultural events, recreation, labor, and even criminal activity, the cultural vitamin of their Mexicanness crosses the border to nourish the Chicano population. Mexicans, legal or otherwise, who enter occupied Mexico and integrate themselves within the local border communities become the Chicanos of tomorrow. Chicanos have learned to be trilingual and tricultural. In order to find accommodation within the white Anglo world, a Chicano must be more Anglo than the host. In order to relate to Mexicans, a Chicano must be as Mexican as they, and in order to build the "other Mexico" in the United States, Chicanos have had to develop their own culture to be themselves among themselves. Herein lies the problem for those ethnic leaders who manipulate the stock of symbols in their culture: How can they create a sense of community? Who is the community? Who is the Chicano?

SEARCHING FOR A LABEL

The search for a self-descriptive label, a self-identifier, has plagued Chicanos for decades. The U.S. government has contributed to the problem. In 1930, the U.S. Bureau of the Census included "Mexican" as a category under "Race." The Census Bureau claimed that this racial category was removed by the 1940 Census due to objections from the Mexican government. In the 1940s the bureau racially classified Mexicans as Caucasians—as white. This classification uncertainty, typified by a U.S. governmental agency, has affected the Chicano community for generations.

Early Chicano organizations had no identity problem. Their organizational names and the names for their movements were in Spanish. It was not until 1927, with the birth of the League of United Latin American Citizens (LULAC), that English was used for an organizational name and that the concept of "Latin American" was first employed. Since that time verbal somersaults have been the order of the day. Chicanos have been described as Spanish-speaking, Spanish, Latin, Indo-Hispanic, Hispanic, Mexican-American, and other similar terms. The question in English, "What are you?", may elicit from the respondent one of these labels, if not simply "American." However, the query in Spanish, "¿Que eres tu?", brings from the respondent only one of two answers: Mexicano or Chicano. From time to time, persons speaking in Spanish will refer to themselves in obvious fashion as "Raza." Chicanos do not have an identity problem when thinking or speaking in Spanish. The problem occurs when Chicanos are forced to interact with an English-speaking white world.

The Chicanos' ideas and culture are transmitted through both the Spanish and English languages. Ideas and thoughts expressed in Spanish, appreciated and digested predominantly by the Spanish-speaking populations, have often been ignored by the mass media and even by academicians. The assumption is sometimes made that Chicanos have neither a historical presence nor an ideological one because of English-hearing ears deaf to Spanish-speaking sounds. The academic myopia comes in large part from self-imposed linguistic and cultural barriers of the monolingual, English-speaking researcher of Chicano speech and communication. Reies Lopez Tijerina generally has spoken in Spanish when addressing audiences. He speaks in English only and mainly for the media and occasionally for college students. Cesar Chavez is fluent in both Spanish and English, and employs Spanish and English effectively with the media, non-Spanish-speaking audiences, college students, and community groups of Chicanos. Rodolfo "Corky" Gonzales speaks predominantly in English and has a beginner's command of Spanish. Consequently, a researcher unskilled in the Spanish language would necessarily ignore all the transmission uttered in Spanish. Only the English statements would constitute the universe of Chicano speech and communication.

THE CENSUS AND LABELING

The labeling of Chicanos has caused many problems, one of them being a Census Bureau error in every count for every decade. The Bureau of the Census estimates that white Americans were undercounted in 1970 by 1.9 percent; black Americans by 7.7 percent; and Chicanos, those native U.S. citizens of Mexican parentage, by 13.8 percent. The bureau also recorded two sets of statistics for this population in the 1970 figures: 9,072,602 persons who were of Spanish origin and 9,589,216 persons who spoke the Spanish language. However, persons with a Spanish surname in the United States totaled 10,114,878. The 1980 census count reflects the same problem of an undercount, even though this last enumeration was the first time an entire national sample was conducted for this population.

Census figures released in late February 1981 placed the number of persons of Hispanic origin at 14,605,883 or 6.4 percent of the total population. Although the persons answering the census questionnaire were personally able to check their preference for an ethnic label, language, and national origin, they were severely undercounted because of faulty mailing lists. The mail lists utilized in the 1980 census were dated at least ten years earlier. Subsequent updates for major metropolitan areas did not alter the basic fault of baseline data. A congressional subcommittee alleged that postal carriers failed to add addresses for new households, particularly in rural areas and apartment dwellings.[6]

The undercount of the Census Bureau and the labeling for the ethnic groups that comprise the "Hispanic" community are of vital concern to Chicano leaders. Numbers are important in intergroup relations with other Spanish-surnamed, Spanish-language subgroups such as Cubans, Puerto Ricans, or the various communities from Central America. Numbers are also important internally to the community to ascertain the native born, the foreign born, the naturalized, the undocumented, and the recent immigrant. Moreover, numbers determine the largesse of government grants as well as charitable and philanthropic contributions to populations in need. Community planning and the allocation of political power are done on the basis of numbers of people. Consequently, the rhetoric of Chicano leaders has increasingly addressed the issue of population counts and related demographic data.

Chicano arguments about numerical strength and majority/minority status are carried in the major dailies and monthly news magazines across the country. Chicanos claim that the Spanish-speaking peoples of the United States will become the largest ethnic minority in the country before the end of the twentieth century, surpassing black America.

The black response to this claim has been prejudiced by hysterical stories in the mass media depicting these gains as "take-overs" of and competition with black gains of the recent past. Efforts are underway among national organizations and leaders to bridge this information gap. The National Council of La Raza recently organized a committee on Hispanic and black concerns, and Reverend Jesse Jackson addressed the issue repeatedly during his 1984 presidential campaign. These two efforts stress the advantages of combined numerical strength. This budding coalition of interests has the potential of coalescing the nation's largest minorities into what could become a powerful economic and political bloc.

Chicano leaders have begun to comment on the real power

of this potential numerical strength. This writer frequently speaks of "Painting the White House Brown," a phrase that instantly produces laughter, cheers, and sustained applause among Chicanos. The hope that Chicanos will one day command significant power from the court house to the White House is a growing realization. The Chicano community is well on its way toward developing, with occasional support from Mexico, a viable economic and political infrastructure within the United States. Armed with growing numerical strength and with the creation of major institutions within the national Chicano community such as the National Council of La Raza, the Mexican-American Legal Defense and Educational Fund, and the Southwest Voter Registration and Education Project, Chicano rhetoric is presently leading to an important new reality. Chicanos are electorally taking power in the Southwest. New Mexico and California are in the forefront of these victories, followed closely by Texas, Colorado, Arizona, and selected regions in the Midwest and Northwest.

THE SPANISH LANGUAGE

The Spanish language is gaining practitioners the world over. In the United States, which is the fourth largest Spanish-speaking country in the world, Chicanos and Mexicanos have various levels of Spanish-language competence. Some are completely literate in Spanish only (resident aliens and new immigrants); some are literate in English and orally literate in Spanish (most Chicanos and Puerto Ricans); others are literate in English with limited or no comprehension of Spanish (mostly urban Chicanos and other Hispanics); and a small but growing number are completely literate in both languages. Regardless of severe budget cuts for bilingual education by President Ronald Reagan ($58 million cut from fiscal year 1982 to 1983), there are notable factors at work to provide the continued acquisition and maintenance of Spanish. We are speaking here not of the public schools, but of the news media, business, and Chicano organizations. As of 1977, forty-one radio stations in the United States broadcast more than 50 percent of their air time in Spanish; by 1984, that number had doubled. Spanish-language television via direct signal and cable access is broadcast throughout the United States. A recent study on consumerism reported that Spanish-speaking residents in the United States earned $51.8 billion in 1980, $30 billion of which they spent on consumer goods. The study concludes: "The potential for dramatically increasing sales by captivating the consumers' attention through advertising is higher in the Hispanic market than in the general market."[7] Furthermore, many Chicano organizations, for example, the National Association of Bilingual Education with its many state affiliates, the National Chicano Studies Association and its many state affiliates, and countless local, regional, and other national groups, all continue to push and practice bilingualism in Spanish and English. Couple these factors with the daily crossing of undocumented Mexicans into the United States, and Spanish will continue its ascendancy as a second, unofficial language in the United States. Concomitantly, there are nativist forces at work to undermine the growth of Spanish-language influence in the United States. In the November 1984 general election in California, the voters passed a proposition to eliminate bilingual materials for the voting process and to make English the official language in the state.

THE SYMBOL OF RELIGION

The religious character and personality of Mexicans and of their descendants in the United States, the Chicanos, is shaped by the dual nature of their origins. Mexicans are at once Indians and Spaniards, while Chicanos are at once Mexicans and Anglos. We could begin with the example of the Aztec goddess, Tonantzin, used by the first Jesuits. Tonantzin, a dark-skinned Indian goddess, lived in a forest sanctuary called Tepeyac. Her name meant "our mother," or *nuestra madre* to the local population. The Spanish conquistador, Hernan Cortez, who came from the borough of Extremadura in Medellin, Spain, brought with him an image of Nuestra Senora de Guadalupe de Extremadura. The ancient Mexicans saw in Cortez's virgin their Tonantzin. Both images had dark skin, dark hair and eyes, high cheekbones, and straight noses. It was no problem for the early missionaries to interchange Tonantzin with the Virgen de Guadalupe. The "miracle" of Our Lady of Guadalupe who appeared to Juan Diego at Tepeyac was the beginning of a formal, religious, reinterpretative interface of native Mexican culture and Spanish, Christian religion. The Mexican legend of Tonantzin in Tepeyac appearing as Nuestra Senora de Guadalupe to a sheepherder in the 1530s is identical to the story of Nuestra Senora de Guadalupe de Extremadura in Spain who likewise appeared to a sheepherder in the early 1400s.[8]

The reverence for the Virgen de Guadalupe, the modern-day Mexican Virgin Mary, is at once the affirmation of an indigenous past and the acceptance of Western Christian symbolism. The Virgin is the mother to whom Mexicans are both siblings and slaves. She is the representative and protector of the Mexican people. The symbol of the Virgin, bathed in sunlight, standing on a half moon, with stars shining over the cactus of the forest in Tepeyac, is prominently displayed not only at religious services in Mexico, but also at public demonstrations of social activities and the Chicanos' political buttons. Every farmworkers' march appears to place the symbol of the Virgen de Guadalupe at the front of the group.

Since the conquest, Mexicans have been Roman Catholic, and since the conquest of 1848, Chicanos, too, have been Catholic. Recently in Mexico and in the United States, however, Protestantism has grown rapidly. Although Catholicism has been a symbol for political ethnic mobilization in Mexico, in the Chicano movement religion has been less important.

Politically influential religious organizations have been emerging in recent years. For example, the Catholic *cursillo* movement of the 1950s, the Encuentro Familiar of the late 1960s and 1970s, Catolicos for La Raza in the 1970s, and most recently, the church sponsored and financed parish-based urban organizations, for example, Communities Organized for Public Service (COPS), United Neighborhood Organization (UNO), and Valley Interfaith, have combined political activities with religious observances. The potential for religion as a symbol of cultural unity and ethnicity is present. In the late 1960s loose associations of Chicano priests and nuns organized themselves under the names of Padres and Hermanas.[9] Originally limited to Chicano clergy whose focus was reform within the Catholic Church, these organizations today extend membership to any one who supports their program. These organizations support many causes other than reform within the Church. Their Affirmative Action Program within the Catholic Church has led to the appointment of more than a dozen Hispanic bishops when formerly there were none. The titular leader of this loose and nebulous amalgam of Catholics is San Antonio's Archbishop Patricio Flores, a Chicano political leader as well as a Catholic officeholder. Archbishop Flores has been the central figure behind the formation of Communities Organized for Public Service (COPS) in San Antonio, Texas. This organization is a new model for urban community organizations based in the parishes. Accomplished community organizer Ernie Cortez is the architect behind these organizations which have successfully married Catholic Church resources with urban Chicano parishioners. The COPS model has been replicated in Los Angeles, Houston, El Paso, and the South Texas Valley.

Archbishop Flores has often been directly involved with Chicano protest actions. In Texas, he has provided support for undocumented persons, the most important civil rights issue for Chicanos. He has stood publicly with Cesar Chavez in support of the Farah strikers, with Chicano garbage collectors on strike, with COPS, and he has spoken out against the Texas Rangers, police brutality, and gerrymandering. He encourages voter registration and participation among Chicanos. The leadership of Archbishop Flores and other bishops, as well as of Padres and of Hermanas, is now looking to unlock the huge capital investments and resources of the Catholic Church for Chicano parish development.

TERRITORY, BORDERS, AND NATIONALITY

The secession of Texas from Mexico in 1821, the invasion of Mexico by the United States in 1846, and the Gadsden Purchase of parts of Arizona all physically altered the geography of Mexico. These events created within the United States the Southwest, or Aztlan as Chicanos refer to the region. Today, every state west of the Mississippi has a sizable Chicano population. In every state of the West, Chicanos are the largest ethnic minority group. Within each state in the West and Southwest every county has a Chicano population. Moreover, Chicanos are the fastest growing ethnic group in the United States. The fertility rate for females of Mexican ancestry is twice that of black and white women.

Prior to 1980 the U.S. Census Bureau limited its enumeration of Chicanos to the Southwest, in accordance with the common stereotype that this population resided only in the Southwest. However, the national count in 1980 and the travels of Chicano leaders outside the United States, which made national news, demonstrated that this community was everywhere. In the 1970s and 1980s Chicanos crossed the border into Mexico and beyond, not just to visit family but also to establish political ties with other peoples. This internationalization of the Chicano community signifies the growing awareness that the Chicano's political destiny is tied not only to the White House and Wall Street, but also to Mexico and the Third World. Consistent with this view, some Chicano internationalists have courted Marxist-Leninist groups whose ideology is firmly rooted in the assumption of an international proletarian struggle.

Today, Chicanos ponder the potential questions of boundary, territory, and nationality along four general lines of thought: (1) Are Chicanos one among many cultural communities in the United States? (2) Are Chicanos a nation within a white/black nation? (3) Are Chicanos the separatists that will form the other Mexico? (4) Are Chicanos an extension of Mexico, *un pueblo sin fronteras* (a people without territorial boundaries)?

IMMIGRATION

Arthur Corwin studied the implications to the United States of immigration from Mexico, Central and South America, and the Caribbean. The findings of the Corwin Report were incorporated into official policy by the Nixon, Ford, and Carter administrations. Massive raids, dragnets, and deportations of Mexicans became the order of the day in the late 1960s and 1970s. Chicanos have felt the brunt of this brutality for years. The Border Patrol of the Immigration and Naturalization Service, second only to the infamous Texas Rangers, represents a gestapo-like police unit for Chicanos. The Border Patrol, *la migra*, is paid to hunt

Mexicans. The "immigration problem" is usually viewed as a Mexican problem and is seldom connected to Canadian immigration. Yet Canada, with a fourth of Mexico's population, has historically exported twice the number of immigrants to the United States than Mexico—approximately 4 million to 2 million.

Immigration issues have become a major concern and priority across the country. In August 1977 President Jimmy Carter outlined the economic and political problems caused by Mexican immigration to this country. The Carter Plan, as it was dubbed, threatened to place the Chicano community as a subclass of residents under constant surveillance and would require that they possess national identification cards. The Carter Plan also unilaterally called for population control programs for women in source countries of Central and South America. More Border Patrol agents were requested for the U.S./Mexico border, and electronic gadgetry was proposed to monitor the border crossings more efficiently.

The following October, just two months after the President had outlined his plan, Chicanos and other Latinos from across the country responded to a call for action against the plan issued by the national chairperson of La Raza Unida party. Every major Chicano and Latino organization and leader, save Lionel Castillo, the commissioner for the Immigration and Naturalization Service, joined in opposition to the Carter Plan. The Carter Plan was defeated in Congress. In the first Reagan Administration immigration bills were again sponsored in Congress, this time by Senator Alan Simpson (R-Wyoming) and Representative Romano Mazzoli (D-Kentucky). The National Council of La Raza and LULAC spearheaded the national opposition against the Simpson-Mazzoli bills. These legislative efforts incorporated many items of the Corwin Report and the Carter Plan. The fight against these bills even reached the Democratic Convention of 1984 as a major issue among the delegates. Democratic party figures such as San Antonio Mayor Henry Cisneros, Denver Mayor Federico Peña, New Mexico Governor Toney Anaya, and hundreds of Hispanic delegates worked out a commitment from Walter Mondale and House Speaker "Tip" O'Neill to oppose the immigration bill's passage in the final days of the congressional session for 1984. The Simpson-Mazzoli bills eventually were defeated.

THE INTERNATIONALIZATION OF THE CHICANO MOVEMENT

Reies Lopez Tijerina first traveled to Mexico City in 1956 searching for information and documentation on the Treaty of Guadalupe Hidalgo. As a result of his search, he established contact with various governmental officials. He even attempted to obtain an interview with the Mexican Secretary of State and President Adolfo Lopez Mateos. Tijerina traveled repeatedly to Mexico beginning in the mid-1950s and finally to Spain in his search for land grant documentation. In his travels he constantly combined his study with the promotion of Chicano land claims to the American Southwest. His activism alarmed both the U.S. and Mexican governments as is evidenced by his deportation from Mexico on the personal orders of President Lopez Mateos in 1964. Undaunted, Tijerina continued his efforts to search for land titles and make the world aware of the land theft in the Southwest.

Similarly, Cesar Chavez and his boycott of grapes internationalized the struggles of the Chicano farmworkers. His brother, Ricardo, spent a great deal of time in England, the Scandinavian countries, and other European countries seeking and obtaining support for the grape boycott of the 1960s. Through Chavez Europeans learned of the plight of Chicano field hands and of the larger struggle of the Chicano community.

During the late 1960s and by the mid-1970s, many students and barrio theatre groups traveled to foreign countries. In his speeches and writing, Rodolfo "Corky" Gonzales frequently alluded to analogous international movements and struggles. His organization, the Crusade for Justice, established viable working relationships with Third World peoples in the United States. El Teatro Campesino and other Chicano artistic groups met in Cali, Colombia, in 1969 at the International Conference of Theatre Groups from the Americas. Chicano and Mexican theatre groups frequently exchange tours in both countries. The subject matter for their presentations continues to be cultural affirmation and aspects of the Chicano movement.

Regional Chicano leaders such as Raul Ruiz of Los Angeles and Carlos Guerra of Robstown, Texas, traveled to Cuba and China in the 1960s. Ricardo Sanchez, the Chicano poet from El Paso, participates regularly in the International Conference of Poets. At the behest of President Carter, national leaders of the American G.I. Forum and LULAC visited Panama in 1977–1978 to lobby for passage of the Panama Canal Treaty. Regardless of their official ties to White House diplomatic strategy, for the Panamanians these individuals represented a heretofore unknown facet of the U.S. ethnic community. In April and May of 1975, a nineteen-member delegation representing the regional leadership of La Raza Unida party was invited to Cuba. This is the only Cuban invitation to date extended to a political party of the United States. In August 1980 a large contingent of Chicano activists, including Juan Jose Peña of the New Mexico Raza Unida party, visited Beirut at the invitation of the Red Crescent, the "Red Cross" of the Palestinian people. Antonio Orendain of the Texas Farmworkers Union has twice journeyed to the Middle East. Frank Shaffer-Corona, the former Chicano Board of Education member in Washington, D.C., also has figured centrally in dialogue and visits to Cuba, Mexico, Quebec, Lebanon, and Iran. In 1984, Mario Obledo, the national president of LULAC, toured Mexico and Cuba and met with their respective heads of state to discuss issues and problems of common concern.

In their attempt to establish advantageous international relations, Chicano individuals and organizations assert, delineate, and advocate a Chicano foreign policy. While the White House has had considerable difficulty presenting a clear and concise policy on international issues, Chicanos have sketched out a sufficiently clear international posture within a framework of six major points: (1) they are individuals desirous of influencing foreign relations on behalf of the Chicano community and are not connected officially with the U.S. government; (2) they search for similar social movements by other peoples; (3) they present the Chicanos' case to the international community; (4) they join with others to oppose U.S. foreign policy on some issues; (5) they actively oppose U.S. immigration policy; and (6) they distance themselves from White House attitudes and values toward Latin America.

This international posture can best be appreciated by analyzing the growing dialogue between Chicano leaders and high-ranking Mexican officials. Prior to 1970, Chicanos and the Mexican President avoided direct contact. However, President Luis Echeverria Alvarez believed that the Third World began territorially within the United States and included non-white peoples in the United States and Europe. This writer and Reies Lopez Tijerina provided form and substance for the beginnings of relations between Chicano groups and the Mexican President. When President Echeverria visited the United States a few months prior to President Richard M. Nixon's reelection victory in 1972, he sought out and made himself available to Chicano leaders and organizations in San Antonio, Chicago, and Los Angeles. From these initial meetings developed a Mexican/Chicano agenda for additional periodic meetings and programs culminating in the establishment of the Comision Mixta de Enlace, or Hispanic Commission as it was called in the United States. This commission was formed by ten Chicano organizations: the American G.I. Forum, LULAC, the National Association of Farmworker Organizations, the Mexican American Legal Defense and Educational Fund, Project SER, the National Council of La Raza, IMAGE, the National Hispanic Forum, the Mexican-American Women's National Association, and a Puerto Rican organization, ASPIRA. The commission met periodically with Mexico's Secretary of Labor during the administration of Jose Lopez Portillo. However, with the election of Miguel de la Madrid Hurtado, the commission has not been utilized as a forum for discussing mutual concerns. The President of Mexico has continued to meet with individual Chicano leaders. In 1984 Mario Obledo, the national president of LULAC, met with both President de la Madrid and Cuban Premier Fidel Castro. The Mexican President is more accessible to Chicanos than is the U.S. president.

THE HISTORICAL BACKGROUND OF CHICANO RHETORIC

The notions of white racial superiority found fertile ground during the nineteenth century. The roots of Anglo racism regarding Mexicans date back to the early 1800s. Of particular impact was the application of Social Darwinism to the imperialist program of territorial expansion and the cultural genocide of non-white peoples. "Manifest Destiny" was the slogan used to support racial determinism. The dime novels of the late nineteenth and early twentieth centuries depict the vicious stereotyping of the Mexican peoples.[10]

Racial attacks, coupled with the physical occupation of Mexican land, have always prompted some Chicanos to resist domination. After the official cessation of violence with the signing of the Treaty of Guadalupe Hidalgo on 2 February 1848 came the unofficial violence associated with conquest. Domination of the inhabitants, oppression and repression of their culture, and colonization of the region have been resisted by the Mexican population. Racist notions among the new governors institutionalized oppression of the Mexican culture and made the Mexican people an exploited class. Total conquest of the borderland, however, has been incomplete.[11]

Early efforts at political participation and social dialogue between the defeated Mexicans in the borderlands (what is now the U.S. Southwest) and the invaders from the North were also frustrated by the linguistic confrontations between the Spanish and English languages. Juan Nepomuceno "Cheno" Cortina, an early Chicano rhetor, exhorted his followers in the mid-1850s to continue the struggle against the United States with arms. In Spanish he called for liberation of a territory, to be designated the Republica del Rio Grande, in the area of south Texas and northern Tamaulipas, Mexico. Similarly, in New Mexico, Diego Archuleta and Antonio Jose Martinez, along with the Taos Pueblo Indians from 1846 to the 1850s, organized groups of insurrectionists to fight off the Anglo invaders. In the 1880s two vigilante organizations, La Mano Negra and Las Gorras Blancas, continued the rebellion against ranchers and railroad men. The Anglos' theft of land from Mexican and Spanish families became the burning issue of these early years. The recovery of these lands and secessionist movements have been constant themes articulated by Chicano leaders.

There are white English-speaking persons who view Mexican Spanish-speaking persons as inferior. Mexicans are viewed as being culturally deficient and are discriminated against because they are different. The Mexicans and their descendants, the Chicanos, remain defeated victims in the eyes of the dominant English-speaking culture. While the "No Mexicans or Dogs Allowed" signs seen in commercial establishments during the first half of this century have been removed, bigotry and institutionalized racism have continued. That racist remarks and hate sheets still abound today should come as no surprise to anyone. Prominent public officials frequently lead the attacks. An example is the infamous statement made in the early 1970s by Superior Court Judge (California) Gerald C. Chargin:

We ought to send you out of the country, send you back to Mexico. You belong in prison for the rest of your life for doing things of this kind. You ought to commit suicide. . . . You are lower than animals and haven't the right to live in organized society . . . just miserable, lousy, rotten people. . . . Maybe, Hitler was right. The animals in our society probably ought to be destroyed because they have no right to live among human beings.[12]

The judge was addressing a thirteen-year-old Chicano charged with incest of his fifteen-year-old sister.

Other examples abound. During February 1980 a federal court case in Houston, Texas, heard arguments on providing educational opportunity to children from Mexico in Texas schools. Federal District Judge Woodrow Seals commented in open court that he had never seen anything of worldwide importance written or published in Spanish.[13] And during the Carter Administration, Charles B. Renfrew, a District U.S. Attorney General, submitted in a law review article his views on discrimination. He wrote the following with regard to Spanish-surnamed Americans:

Today, we could probably gain general societal agreement that the discriminatory behavior of the white majority is quite directly responsible for the disadvantaged position of the American Indian and the American Black. . . . The history of extensive and long-lived de jure discrimination distinguishes those minorities from all others in the U.S. . . . The difficulty of this inquiry is illustrated by reference to the Spanish-surnamed Americans. How do we evaluate the claim of this group to preferential treatment, in light of the more regionalized, less pervasive, but clearly discernible, prejudice which they have suffered? The fact of much prejudice is undisputed. Yet, has it been the pervasive de jure and nationwide discrimination suffered by Blacks and Native Americans? The greater numbers of these Americans either came to this country voluntarily or are the descendants of those who did. . . . A national rectification principle must perhaps, fairly and logically, be limited to American Indians and Blacks.[14]

CHICANO IDEOLOGY: THE LULAC EXAMPLE OF ASSIMILATIONIST THOUGHT

Pedro Hernandez and Maria Latigo married in 1915 and settled in Hebbronville, Texas.[15] They soon heard of Feliciano Flores from San Antonio, who, together with two of his four sons, Feliciano and Jose Angel, had organized a civic group of Mexicans called Los Hijos de Texas. In 1918 Pedro and Maria moved to San Antonio because World War I had begun and Pedro was waiting for conscription. In San Antonio Pedro and Maria studied Los Hijos de Texas and another group being formed, La Orden de Hijos de America. They were curious about these organizations and their goals because

nacio en el cerebro de mi esposa y el mio, la idea de organizar un grupo civico para despertar mas y mas la conciencia civica de los nuestros . . . a fin de aumentar el numero de votantes en las contiendas electorales y asi hacernos buen uso de los derechos civicos. Llevaremos al poder a elementos reponsables de nuestro pueblo.

[born in the mind of my wife and I, was the idea of organizing a civic group to awaken more and more the civic consciousness of our own . . . toward the end of increasing the number of voters in the elections, and thereby making good use of civic rights. We shall take to power those responsible elements of our community.]

In 1924 they joined La Orden Hijos de America and began a life of social activism which lasted through the 1970s.

During their early years in La Orden another organization surfaced in south Texas. On 14 August 1927, Alonso Perales of Alice, Texas, had called an organizational meeting to form the

Liga de Ciudadanos Latino Americanos from among the chapters of La Orden de Hijos de America and Los Hijos de Texas.[16] Alonso Perales was able to attract members, and within two years at a meeting in Corpus Christi the Liga changed its name to League of United Latin American Citizens (LULAC). The local La Orden chapter from San Antonio refused membership into the league and chose instead to alter its name to La Orden Caballeros de America. Pedro and Maria Hernandez were members of the original Orden and were among the dissidents at the LULAC founding. They explained: "No tienen lo que yo mas nos interesaba, actividad civica y fraternal para ambos sexos. Otros grupos excluyen a sus mujeres, forman auxiliares de mujeres. Para me (Pedro) los sexos son diferentes pero iguales en derechos." ("They didn't have what I mostly was interested in, fraternal and civic activity for both sexes. Other groups exclude their women, form auxiliary women's groups. To my view, the sexes are different but equal in their rights.")

They also strongly disagreed with the LULAC preamble and the implication inherent in the name change from the Spanish to English: "La palabra 'Americano', el verdadero Americanismo es de todos los hijos de America, no importa su color, mi naconalidad, o raza. Yo siempre que hablo digo Mexicano o Etudianense en lugar de Mexico Americano. La palabra que viene primero es 'Americano'." ("The word American, the real Americanism, belongs to the children of America, regardless of their color, nationality or race. When I speak I always say American Mexican or United States, instead of Mexican American. The first word that should be first is American.") Clearly, their nationalistic perspective, together with their emphasis on equality for the sexes, their preference for electoral activity, and their Pan Americanism, were in complete contradiction of the LULAC preamble and philosophy.

LULAC advocated education as the panacea for social ills. Early LULAC leaders and followers agreed that total assimilation into the Anglo-American culture and society would eliminate discrimination against "Latin Americans." LULAC's founder, Alonso Perales, and his colleagues, Bernardo Garcia, Luz Sanchez, Jose T. Canales, Carlos Castañeda, Eluterio Escobar, and Henry Guerra, among others, tirelessly developed strategies to attack the lack of educational opportunities for Chicanos. For example, in 1934 Eluterio Escobar of San Antonio formed a committee, La Liga Por Defensa Escolar, to protest conditions in Mexican schools located in the westside barrio of the city. Rallies and street marches were the tactics employed by the Liga. The superintendent of schools for the State Board of Education, L. L. Woods, attended a rally at which he was presented with a list of grievances. The list included the lack of adequate classroom space, lack of classroom heat, lack of windowshades and drapes, abnormally high student/teacher ratios (130 students per teacher), and lack of standard, inhabitable facilities. Among the nine prominent speakers at the LULAC-sponsored rally was Maria Hernandez. She was the only one to speak in Spanish. She said: "Señores padres de familia, por favor, ponganse de pie para protestar las injusticias en las escuelas." ("Gentlemen, parents, please stand to protest the injustices in our schools.") As the crowd rose to the call, she turned to Superintendent Woods and continued in Spanish: "Los hijos de ellos no tuvieron culpa de nacer con ojos negros, pelo cafe y no con ojos azules. Todos somos apoyados por el pabellon de las barras y estrellas. Yo quiero que usted tome esta gestion del pueblo como protesta y disgusto de las condiciones pesimas." ("Their children were not at fault for being born with black eyes and brown hair and not with blue eyes. We are all supported by the stripes and stars of the flag. I want you to take this gesture of this community as a protest and disgust over the terrible conditions.")

The crowd roared its approval with applause and whistles. However, it also demanded of the speaker an English translation so that the school authority could understand its protest as articulated by Maria Hernandez. Santiago Tafolla translated immediately. Before Maria could continue with her remarks, the superintendent interrupted the proceedings. He promised to appoint a commission to investigate the complaints and, if the allegations were found to be true, to remedy the problems.

LULAC soon broadened its efforts, fighting prostitution; publishing an English-language newspaper, *LULAC News*; introducing litigation against the segregation of Mexican children in the public schools; and developing an early bilingual, pre-kindergarten educational program, "the little school of 400."

Between the founding of LULAC and the emergence of another major organization, the American G.I. Forum of 1948, countless other groups formed whose ideological imprint is with us today—for example, the Unity Leagues, the Catholic Church's Bishops Committee for the Spanish Speaking, and the Community Service Organization (CSO). These assimilationist groups had the following characteristics:

1. Their organizational names were changed from the Spanish to English or were initially in English.

2. They adopted Anglo labels for their ethnicity, that is, Latin Americans, Spanish-Americans, and Spanish-Speaking.

3. They permitted membership of women and youth in separate auxiliary groups.

4. They held conventions, required paid membership dues, and followed *Robert's Rules of Order* for their parliamentary rules.

5. English was the official language of the organization.

6. They sought to adopt Anglo middle-class values as a substitute for their Mexican traditions. U.S. citizenship was made a prerequisite for membership.

7. The founders and prominent leaders were white collar professionals.

8. The rituals of the organizations and the membership strongly identified with symbols of U.S. patriotism, that is, the flag, the Pledge of Allegiance, and so on.

The assimilationists believed that Anglicization would lead to acceptance by the dominant group and that subsequent entry into the Anglo middle-class world would inevitably follow. Thus, these early leaders and followers believed that speaking English without an accent, obtaining an education, being effusively patriotic, and adopting many trappings of Anglo America would solve the social, political, and economic problems of the Chicano people. In other words, they accepted the notion that their culture and heritage was the cause of their problems. Their solution was to change themselves to be mirrors of the dominant society.

CHICANO IDEOLOGY: INSURRECTIONIST
THOUGHT AND ARMED STRUGGLE

In contrast to the assimilationist strain in Chicano ideological thought is that which supports insurrection and armed struggle. Incipient movements such as those led by Juan "Cheno" Cortina sought to seize territory for the founding of a new nation. Cortina fought a twenty-year war with the military forces of both Mexico and the United States. His army briefly controlled the area between Brownsville and Corpus Christi until the 1890s. Cortina established a political movement complete with intelligence-gathering units, and he organized a cadre of families along the border as logistic support units and as fighting troops. He made appeals to the masses through printed leaflets, newspapers, and public speeches, all in Spanish.

In the 1860s, near El Paso, the Salt Wars took place between local Mexicans and greedy, monopolistic Anglo entrepreneurs. These Anglo businessmen came upon the area's salt beds, discovered that the property was not registered properly at the local court house, filed their own land claim with the deed/ records office, and took physical possession of the salt beds. They built a fence around the property and began to charge the locals for the taking of salt. The native population revolted at this theft of community property, and their armed struggles lasted a decade. In the end, with armed support from Texas Rangers and the state authorities, the Anglos won.

In April 1889 in New Mexico, Las Gorras Blancas, a vigilante group, also engaged in open rebellion, fighting the land-grabbing tactics of encroaching white squatters. After years of range violence and little success, Las Gorras Blancas opted for an additional strategy of independent electoral activity under the banner of El Partido del Pueblo. At the turn of the century yet another political party emerged, El Partido Mexicano Liberal. The Mexican Liberal party was organized in Mexico six years prior to the outbreak of the revolution in 1910. The founders of the party, the Magon brothers, had been exiled to the United States by the dictator, General Porfirio Diaz; operating from various points in the United States, Ricardo and Enrique Magon promoted their revolutionary effort. They established organizational bases in various cities with local populations of Mexican ancestry such as San Antonio, Los Angeles, and El Paso, where many Chicanos embraced this movement. The newspapers of the party, *Regeneracion* and *El Centenario*, were effective propaganda organs written in Spanish. While the organizing efforts of the Magon brothers were aimed at fomenting revolution in Mexico, their audience was more interested in their ideas on working-class solidarity, the exploitative nature of capitalism, Mexican working conditions, foreign investments in Mexico, and the Diaz dictatorship. Ramon Gonzalez, a custodian at the Brooks County Court House between 1908 and 1917, recalled the organizational meeting of La Estrella Solitaria in Falfurrias, Texas. The meeting had been called by former *sediciosos* (seditionists) from the Magon movement who urged the local residents to engage in armed struggle against the Anglos to liberate their lands and form the Republic of Texas. Labor unrest among the Mexican immigrants and Chicanos continued to figure prominently in the social activism of the next five decades. During the last two decades we have witnessed the efforts of Chicano/Mexican labor in the Farah strike, the Farm Labor Organizing Committee in Ohio, the Texas Farm Worker Union, the Arizona Farmworkers Union, and, of course, the campaign of Cesar Chavez.

Another ideological movement that emerged in the late 1930s was the unorganized, unstructured, yet highly disciplined and far-reaching, Pachuco Movement. Originating in El Paso, exemplifying an almost purely existentialist philosophy, the Pachucos rebelled against both Anglo and Mexican cultural norms. They created the first Chicano counter-culture, and in so doing they created a new dress code, the Zoot Suit, and new speech patterns, appearance, and behavior unlike any previously known in the Chicano community. This counter-culture movement attracted the wrath of local police and the military community in southern California and across the Southwest. Internal community violence was blamed on the Pachucos, and so they found themselves the victims of violent police and military repression and sensationalist journalism by the Hearst newspaper chain. In the Sleepy Lagoon Case of August 1942 in Los Angeles, blatant judicial bias was shown against the Pachucos. All the members of the 38th Street Club, twenty-four Chicanos, were arrested and collectively charged with the murder of a fellow member, Jose Diaz. The trial resulted in the conviction of seventeen members. Their distinctive dress, speech, and Mexican ancestry had also been placed on trial and had resulted in a finding of guilty of basic un-Americanism. After they served two years of their sentences at San Quentin, their convictions were overturned by a higher appellate court. A year later, in June 1943, police and military riots erupted in the Mexican section of east Los Angeles. Again, the riots gave license to the military police, sailors, marines, and the local police to assault young Chicanos dressed in the Pachuco garb of the day. Filipino and black youths were also among those attacked. Recently, this dark chapter of Anglo/Chicano relations was made public with the successful stage production in 1978 and feature-length movie, *Zoot Suit*, in 1981.

THE CHANGING OF THE IDEOLOGICAL GUARD

The more recent emergence of student and youth groups, both in and out of school, was as much a surprise as the emergence of the Pachucos. Chicano youth, farmworkers, urban poor, women generally, and rural farmworkers began searching for new leaders and an action agenda in the early years of the 1960s. Traditional leaders had excluded these important sectors of the Chicano community from equal participation in their organizations. The predominantly Chicano male groups identified only with their white male counterparts, but the criteria of Anglo organizational models alienated the masses of Chicanos. Moreover, the poor, urban and rural, young and old, male and female, student and worker, could not financially afford the cost of membership and participation. The no-host cocktails, luncheons and dinners, conventions, and financial contributions excluded the least able to pay. Furthermore, because of age and sex, youth and women were relegated to lesser organization roles. Those under twenty-one years of age were excluded totally from participation until they attained majority status.

The traditional leaders excluded many Chicanos from effective participation in another important way. The leadership of assimilationist organizations espoused dogmatic adherence to the rigid, defined practices of Anglo associations often affiliated with the Democratic party; that is, procedural rules of conduct and order were copied from other Anglo organizations. For example, there has been and continues to be an insistence on the passing of carefully worded resolutions at conferences. It is assumed that resolution-passing demonstrates unanimity of thought and implies group action. Chicano conferences pass countless important resolutions, but seldom deliver or mobilize support for action on those issues. The Chicano masses remain indifferent because they were neither consulted nor advised of any planned action. These conventions and resolutions were seen as paper tigers by those being addressed in the resolutions. The traditional organizations also named prominent white male politicians as keynote speakers for their banquets and dinners, ignoring fellow members, leaders, and other distinguished figures from the Chicano or Mexicano community. Hence, the implication was that the Chicano community had no "heroes" among its own residents and that only white politicians were qualified to address and solve the community's problems.

The rise of Cesar Chavez and Reies Lopez Tijerina gave the disaffected Chicanos a choice of different leaders. These two men represented the mainstream of the disaffected. Both men were migrant farmworkers, and both spoke in Spanish of the need for independent action against the Anglo system. Chavez called for a union of farmworkers, while Tijerina sought to recover the land titles which the New Mexicans had lost to Anglos. Next came the rise of Rodolfo "Corky" Gonzales and Jose Angel Gutierrez. Both of these men embarked on a course to legitimize Chicanismo, an operational working definition of Chicano culture. In their speeches, these men utilized new words to give life to the social protest movement of the 1970s. These words—Chicano, Aztlan, La Raza, La Causa, Huelga, Carnalismo, for example—broke with assimilationist thought because they set up an ideological framework of action against the Anglo system. The Chicano slogans called for goals that would result in independently created Chicano social institutions. The words and slogans became self-identifiers that represented pride, cultural identity, political militancy, and concerted, collective action. The young, the women, and the poor saw themselves as the authors of their own advocacy and destiny.

"Chicano" became a call for excluded people to band together and challenge, first, the U.S. cultural ethos and, second, the elder statesmen of the Chicano community such as Hector Garcia of the American G.I. Forum, U.S. Senator Joseph Montoya (D-New Mexico), and U.S. Representative Henry Gonzalez. Echoing the words of "Corky" Gonzales and Gutierrez, activists began calling for Chicanismo and Carnalismo as the mode of behavior for proper cultural nationalism. Young Chicanos began accepting the concept proposed in "El Plan de Aztlan" of a Chicano nation within the United States. This flirtation with separatism and nationhood had its origins in the resistance movements of Juan Cortina, Catarino Garza, Aniceto Pizaña, and the Magon brothers.

POLITICAL PARTIES

The efforts of La Raza Unida party in the 1970s have been recently analyzed and interpreted in the context of the history of Anglo third-party electoral movements in the United States. Chicano efforts to build an ethnic political party date back a century and a half to Juan Nepomuceno Cortina. In a petition to the U.S. Congress, Cortina called for a separate territory to be known as the Republica del Rio Grande. He asked for the formation and appointment of a military government to include a governor, secretary of state, judges, district attorneys, and marshalls. He proposed that rights of appeal from the territorial courts come before the U.S. Supreme Court. The territorial assembly would send a delegate to the U.S. Congress. He also demanded that the laws of Texas applicable to real estate be held in abeyance until other laws could be enacted by their own legislature. Cortina's petition created great concern in Texas and led to massive violence.

In the 1880s another Chicano, Catarino Garza, continued the fight for the creation of a separate nation in south Texas. Garza, who was in the Cortina movement until his death in 1891, was best known for his guerrilla attacks in the Rio Grande Valley and the Winter Garden area of Texas, around Carrizo Springs and Crystal City.

During the summer of 1890 disaffected Chicano Democrats and Republicans together with Las Gorras Blancas met in Las Vegas, New Mexico, to form a political party called El Partido del Pueblo Unido. The Partido expressed opposition to Republican party bossism and wanted resolution of their land grant titles. By not adjudicating these claims, it said, local courts were harming Chicano landowners dispossessed of their land. The Partido also demanded free public education for Hispanos. The party's first convention was held in the fall of 1890, with some sixty representatives from area precincts attending. The Partido carried San Miguel County in the elections of 1890 and 1892. In 1894 it allied itself with the national Populist party and lost its ethnic identity and name.

The organizational efforts of Ricardo and Enrique Magon began in 1904, when they organized the Mexican Liberal party in St. Louis, Missouri. While the Magonistas plotted the revolution in Mexico, local Chicano followers such as Aniceto Pizaña and Luis de la Rosa began organizing a seditionist movement designed to overthrow the U.S. government and to establish an independent Chicano nation in the Southwest. Under the leadership of Pizaña and de la Rosa, the *sediciosos* continued to foment a revolution in Texas. In 1915 they proclaimed the "Plan de San Diego" which called for Texas, California, New Mexico, Arizona, and Colorado to comprise an independent Chicano nation governed by a Supreme Revolutionary Congress. They proposed similar nations for black people and Indians. The capital of the new Chicano nation would be Sante Fe, New Mexico. The "Plan de San Diego" was not successful, and the *sediciosos* ended their efforts around 1920.

The next effort to build a political party surfaced in New Mexico in 1968. Under the leadership of Reies Lopez Tijerina after his return from the Poor People's Campaign, the Board of Elders, La Mesa Cosmica of the Alianza de Pueblos Libres, voted to form the Partido Constitucional del Pueblo. The founding convention, held on 4 August 1968 in Albuquerque, nominated Tijerina for governor and Jose Alfredo Maestas for lieutenant governor. This party called for mandatory bilingual education, a restoration of the Indo-Hispano culture, an independent civilian police review board, the lowering of the voting age to eighteen, and the settlement of all land claims. The party remained on the ballot and participated in New Mexico politics until 1970.

It is notable that the three political parties described above, as well as La Raza Unida which was founded on 17 January 1970 in Crystal City, Texas, were all named in Spanish. La Raza Unida party enjoyed greater organizational success than did the previous parties.[17] At its national convention in September 1972 in El Paso, Texas, representatives and delegates from eighteen states and the District of Columbia attended. The party fielded candidates in Michigan, Wisconsin, Illinois, Colorado, New Mexico, California, Arizona, Texas, and the District of Columbia. Repeated efforts to obtain ballot status in Arizona and California failed. The party's major electoral victories were scored in Texas and the District of Columbia. La Raza Unida party has not fielded candidates in any partisan election in any state since 1980, however, not even in its base of origin, Texas. The party is now practically defunct and has only a handful of adherents in the San Francisco area and the San Fernando Valley. The overwhelming majority of its leadership and membership have joined other political movements, especially the Democratic party.

The tactical value of independent, electoral, political activity has been to organize and mobilize the masses of Chicanos for concerted political action. Voter participation has given the Chicano leverage and political clout from the local city hall level to the White House. The ethnic-based political parties have all made appeals to the identity, language, and national origin of Chicanos. La Raza Unida, for example, was not only a name for the party but also a slogan with a call to action: ethnic group unity.

STATES OF IDEOLOGICAL DEVELOPMENT: THE POSTPONEMENT

It is estimated that 1 million Mexicans crossed the Rio Grande into the United States during the Mexican Revolution. These political refugees thought their stay in the United States would be temporary, for they fully intended to return to Mexico as soon as the violence ended. But when the revolution and its equally violent aftermath continued into 1930, the days turned to years. Meanwhile, the first generation of U.S.-born children came into its majority, and still the parents did not abandon their dream of returning to Mexico. The Immigration and Naturalization Service reports that the time from a Mexican immigrant's first arrival in the United States to the day he or she seeks citizenship is thirty years, which represents the longest tenure for any immigrant group.[18] These political refugees earned a living and continued to raise their families while in the United States, and today they are the grandparent, senior citizen group of resident aliens. These grandparents postponed instilling in their U.S.-born children the need to claim their civil rights. They reasoned that this was not "home" and that they were going home to Mexico after the revolution. Unfortunately, circumstances forced the postponement of their return.

By the 1940s and 1950s, the first generation of U.S.-born Chicanos became parents themselves. They were the migrant generation of seasonal farm laborers traveling annually to the northern states in search of work. While in Michigan, Ohio, Iowa, Minnesota, Nebraska, Idaho, and Oregon, they did not think of protesting social injustice either; they were going home to Texas or California at the season's end. These parents also socialized their children to accept exclusion and differential treatment from the dominant society. Beginning in the 1960s, however, these parents began settling out of the migrant stream with their second- and third-generation Chicano children. These children did not share their grandparents' dream of returning to Mexico or their parents' dream of returning to the Southwest: they were at home in the northern states. Overwhelming numbers of Chicanos abandoned farm labor for blue and white collar occupations beginning in the 1960s. From this current generation of adults came the militant activists of the 1960s and 1970s who did not care to postpone social protest.

THE IDEOLOGY OF THE 1960s

Reies Lopez Tijerina was the Chicanos' single most provocative figure in the decade of resistance.[19] His leadership in the

Alianza de Pueblos Libres focused on the rights of Indo-Hispanics to their land. He advocated armed self-defense of Chicano cultural and property rights and he blamed the Anglo socioeconomic system for the misery of Chicanos in New Mexico and the Southwest. The rise of Tijerina and the land recovery movement signaled the emergence of a new style of social activism by Chicanos in the 1960s.

Tijerina contributed to Chicano ideology through his actions and rhetoric. He believes the following:

1. Chicanos are Indo-Hispanos, a new breed of people forged from an Indian union with Spanish blood. Tijerina has popularized the notion that the Chicanos' baptismal papers as a people are to be found in the Leyes de los Reinos de la Indias, documents that legitimized marriages between Spaniards and Native American women.

2. The land is the Chicanos' heritage and future. Tijerina believes that without land a people are nomads and that the land grab dating to the 1848 period forced the Chicano community into migrancy.

3. Chicanos must fight for the land or die trying. Tijerina has repeatedly called for the internationalization of the struggle. He insistently holds the Mexican government accountable for defending the interests of Mexican descendants in the United States. Tijerina has reached out to Spain, Mexico, various Arab states, and the United Nations in a lobbying effort to obtain support for his land recovery movement. He has offered the Chicano history of exploitation to the world as proof of the hypocrisy of the U.S. government.

4. Chicanos are protected by international law in addition to local law. Tijerina believes that treaties that ended the hostilities between the United States and Mexico are more important than local laws and more applicable. He points out that the supreme laws of the United States are those laws passed by Congress, the decisions of the Supreme Court, and the treaties ratified by the U.S. Senate.[20]

Cesar Chavez's greatest contribution to Chicano ideology was to give substance, form, and structure to his oft-repeated phrase, "¡Si Se Puede!" Chavez gave the Chicano social movement a living symbol of hope, righteousness, simplicity, and non-violence. Organizationally, he legitimized the alliance between Chicanos and non-Chicanos in the work for La Causa of Chicanos;

he recruited the Roman Catholic clergy, long unconcerned with the material needs of Chicanos, into his ranks of activists; and he built his sphere of influence with the use of cultural symbols. In order to bring the Catholic church and its followers into the streets, fields, and public places in support of his Huelgas, he brought the Virgen de Guadalupe out from the church sanctuary to the front of his marches. His leadership forged a hegemony among Chicano groups across the nation. Many other groups of social protest accepted his tactics in building a labor union, notably pickets, rallies, marches, demonstrations, consumer boycotts, theatre skits, poster art, political buttons, and campus speechmaking to raise money.

Together with his United Farmworkers of America, Chavez has time and again faced impossible odds in realizing his goals. He has clearly demonstrated that an organized and mobilized Chicano group can bring a formidable economic and political opposition to the bargaining table, and that an organization can minister to the needs of its own. The union of farmworkers has an array of impressive social programs for its membership, a credit union, health clinics, alternative schools, hiring halls, housing, radio communications, and many other programs. Chavez has successfully combined his dual leadership roles as labor leader for Chicano and Filipino farm laborers and as movement leader/symbol for Chicano organizations.

Rodolfo "Corky" Gonzales, on the other hand, has been the figure behind a cultural renaissance among Chicano youth. From his base in Denver he began coalescing youth in national conferences which he originated and directed. His contribution to Chicano ideology gained national recognition through his poem *Yo Soy Joaquin* and through "El Plan de Aztlan" drafted at the first youth conference in 1967. He founded the Crusade for Justice and actively pursued the incorporation of socialist thought into nationalist goals. He was the first Chicano leader of this generation to reach beyond the U.S. borders intellectually for ideas, speaking to Chicanos about issues in the Third World, international socialism, immigration, and revolution. An outspoken critic of Democratic party politics, having previously been an officeholder in that party, Gonzales became the symbol of independent political action. He demanded community control of local facilities, services, and institutions, and in 1966 at the Crusade for Justice his organization began an alternative education program from pre-kindergarten to higher education. He symbolized the urban alienated Chicano with poor Spanish-speaking skills who thirsted for cultural reinforcement. He bridged the communication gap between barrio youth and *batos locos* (modern day Pachucos), low riders (car club enthusiasts), college kids, high school dropouts, and Vietnam veterans. He legitimized the Chicano movement to all the youth and convinced them it was their movement.

This writer's contribution to ideology came first in the area of educational opportunity and electoral strategy for Chicanos.[21] During the early years of the Mexican-American Youth Organization (MAYO), countless school strikes were carried out. MAYO attacked the educational system for failing to provide Chicanos with a quality educational experience. The leadership of MAYO demanded a curriculum that reflected the Chicano presence and experience. MAYO called for Chicano personnel at all levels of the educational institution. From this aggressive program, MAYO learned to organize students and parents. In the subsequent school strikes of the late 1960s, MAYO organized voter registration drives, led consumer boycotts of businesses related to Board of Education trustees, and recruited Chicano candidates for local school board elections. By then, MAYO leaders firmly believed that the local schools ought to be under the control of Chicano students, parents, and residents. Electoral success followed on the heels of successful school walkouts.

La Raza Unida party, born one week after the first complete victory for boycotting Chicano students in January 1970, was created to fill the requirements of partisan elections because city and school board elections in Texas were non-partisan. The new political party had the distinct advantage of being an ethnic organization whose members spoke in Spanish, directed its program, determined its agenda, and served its unique purposes exclusively. The party's electoral success brought it national mass media attention.

The Chicano community in Crystal City had demanded bilingual education, personnel changes, curriculum revision to reflect Chicano contributions, and Chicano control of the school board. These demands were typical of those made in thirty-nine other school strikes that occurred in Texas between 1967 and 1970. Across other states, in the cities of Denver, Los Angeles, El Paso, Kalamazoo, and Chicago, Chicano students propelled these issues from the classrooms into the streets. The demand for educational opportunities came from the children being denied rather than from their parents, and so leadership on this issue came from the ranks of the students, not the parents or the traditional leaders.

Education has always been a major concern of Chicano leaders. At the time of *mutualistas* (mutual benefit societies), individuals in barrios and colonias organized store-front schools for Chicano children. These early childhood programs were bilingual and bicultural; English was taught as a second language, however. These programs were precursors for LULAC's "little school of 400" and the War on Poverty's Head Start. Demands for public education and a bilingual curriculum had been articulated by many Chicano leaders for many years, but it took the Chicano children to push the issue to the battlefront of the civil rights movement.

Urban youth provided fertile ground for "Corky" Gonzales's ideological framework of cultural nationalism. He rallied disaffected rural, urban, and collegiate youth into social action aimed at paralyzing the public schools. His rationale was simple. If Chicanos could not get access to a quality education, why should anyone else? Gonzales not only demanded bilingual, bicultural education but also the constituents' control of the very institutions that provided such a program. His calls for political action were echoed by other influential Chicanos across the nation. Among these regional leaders were Raul Ruiz (Los Angeles), Armando Navarro (San Bernardino), Angel Moreno (Chicago), Olga Villa (South Bend, Indiana), Jane Gonzalez (Michigan), Alfredo Gutierrez (Arizona), Juan Jose Peña (New Mexico), Reymundo Marin (Washington), and Lupe Anguiano (Texas).

The rise of youth organizations during the 1960s and 1970s was due largely to their political maturation. They saw lack of educational opportunities at all levels, and they opposed further military involvement in Vietnam. Rosalio Muñoz, a former student body president at UCLA, organized the first Chicano moratorium against the war. On 15 November 1969 he heard "Corky" Gonzales speak at an anti-war rally in San Francisco. Among the 250,000 people present at this demonstration were several other Chicano student activists from Los Angeles. Gonzales's words on the issue propelled these students to call for a National Chicano Draft Conference. At this conference, plans were laid for the first of several moratoria against the war. The first moratorium was held on 20 December 1969 in Los Angeles, and a second followed in a matter of months. Other moratoria were soon held in other cities in the Southwest. These efforts culminated in the National Chicano Moratorium on 29 August 1970 in east Los Angeles. More than 25,000 marchers came to this anti-war demonstration.

The anti-war posture of Chicano youth presented a clear affront to the mainstream thinking of such organizations as the American G.I. Forum and LULAC. These traditional groups have been proud of the record of valor reflected in the disproportionate number of Congressional Medal of Honor winners from the Chicano community. To some Chicanos, proven patriotism has been a precondition for demanding procedural justice from the society. Many older leaders seemed to say that death in battle on behalf of the United States made it possible for the living to seek concessions from society. The youth of this generation questioned the validity of that supposition and rejected the "red-baiting" tactics directed at their protests. The youth counter-argued that patriotism called for opposition to the war in Vietnam, not blind obedience to the White House. The youth pointed out that social domestic spending was being deferred to support more military expenditures and that dying for the flag was nonsense. They contrasted the cultural genocide being inflicted on Chicanos by the same flag-wavers who were calling for greater involvement in Southeast Asia.

This writer, in his role as lead organizer of the Crystal City walkout and founder of La Raza Unida party, became the architect of the national movement for the electoral independence of the Chicano voter. What began as a tactical effort to circumvent Texas Democratic party politics soon became nationally for Chicanos their electoral arm of the movement. This development coincided with earlier notions beginning in 1960 among traditional organizations, namely LULAC, that the Chicanos' growing political clout would soon make this minority the balance of power between contending Democrats and Republicans in the Southwest.

The building of La Raza Unida party was not accomplished without power struggles. The direction of the party became the central debate at the first national convention. The delegates personalized the question of direction by asking that a national leader for the party be chosen from either Rodolfo "Corky" Gonzales or Jose Angel Gutierrez. Gutierrez won the election. Gonzales offered the delegates the classic, traditional Marxist position that La Raza Unida party ought to be a vanguard, elite, revolutionary vehicle for the masses of the Spanish-speaking community within the United States. Gutierrez, on the other hand, proposed a pragmatic and strictly electoral approach to organizing the Chicano community.

La Raza Unida's primary contribution was to break the Chicano's traditional allegiance to the Democratic party. In many rural and some urban areas, the party obtained victories that gave Chicanos effective control of local school boards, city governments and court houses. Their success at the ballot box and the attraction of independent electoral action prompted the major parties to recruit and identify with local and regional Chicano leaders within their own parties. The strong, unique vocal stance of La Raza Unida party in promoting Chicano activism, cultural nationalism, and international solidarity with the global struggles of other people in the Third World gave its members a heretofore unknown feeling of self-determination. Chicanos were in control of their own political affairs and could manage such a task. The party's militancy and success focused attention on the possibilities of a separatist movement by Chicanos in the United States.

Today La Raza Unida party is dead, and the reason is not difficult to find. The party has followed the traditional trajectory of other third-party movements in the Chicano community. The youth from MAYO who were in the forefront of La Raza Unida party have been lured, co-opted, elected, and recruited by other political movements. The issues raised by La Raza Unida party, such as bilingual education, permanent voter registration, Chicano studies programs, bilingual ballots, community control of barrio institutions, and equal opportunity for Chicanos, for example, have all been incorporated into actual programs. These once radical demands are today moderate ongoing activities. Many activists from La Raza Unida party are major officials of the major parties, with some members figuring prominently in the presidential campaigns of 1980 and 1984. Other former members occupy visible and powerful positions as public officials in Congress, state governments, court houses, and city halls.

The process of catering to the Chicano voter as an interest group because of its growing electoral strength is the irreversible legacy of La Raza Unida party. It spoke of Chicano power in real terms of votes and positions of power when its numbers were few and its impact was minimal. Today, Chicanos are converting that potential power into greater benefits.

THE POWER BROKERS IN THE 1980s

With his New Deal programs, Franklin Delano Roosevelt sought to reincorporate large numbers of the population into the mainstream of society through the use of government programs. Both John F. Kennedy and Lyndon B. Johnson made additional attempts to reach the disaffected with the New Frontier and the War on Poverty, respectively. With his New Federalism Richard M. Nixon added to the role of the national government at the local level, particularly with his program of revenue sharing. These four governmental programs have contributed to the rise of the Chicano power broker. This new figure, who depends on governmental grants and foundation dollars, has become a new political leader among Chicanos because of his or her money-raising ability. Patronage has emerged out of federal programs and foundation grants.

During the 1960s and 1970s, almost every idea that came from a Chicano could apparently find funding. Local leaders began to finance their community work from grants. In time, those who provide services to Chicanos created four major national institutions: the National Council of La Raza, the Mexican-American Legal Defense and Educational Fund, the Southwest Voter Registration and Education Program, and the Secretariat for Hispanic Affairs. The first three organizations depend totally for their major sources of funds on foundation sources and government grants. The last-named is a wholly subsidized extension of the U.S. Catholic Church Bishops. None of these major organizations is directly accountable to the Chicano community. While their services are sorely needed and probably can only be provided through philanthropic support,[22] the rise of these major institutions has had a chilling effect on local grass-roots movements. Local and regional organizational efforts cannot compete against these giant organizations in terms of resources, capabilities, programs, or legitimacy. The major organizations serve as gatekeepers to private monies, for their advice and counsel are more readily accepted than those offered by local initiatives. Geographically, except for the voter project, these institutions are located outside of the population concentrations of Chicanos. Moreover, these institutions do not rely on Chicano boards of directors for policy formulation, and among their corporate heads are some Chicanos and non-Chicanos. Consequently, the advocacy role of these entities is limited to issues arbitrarily selected by their Chicano executive directors. These executive directors and the members of the boards are not interested in cultivating and engendering local leadership, much less patronizing budding social protest movements. They have the mistaken idea that competition will diminish their central role as brokers. Without local and regional grass-roots community efforts at social change, there is little need for major institutions. The Chicano power brokers have ushered in the era of community representation by salaried proxies.

NOTES

1. Claudio Veliz, *The Centralist Tradition in Latin America* (Princeton, N.J.: Princeton University Press, 1980).

2. See Clifford Geertz, "The Integrative Revolution: Primordial Sentiments and Civil Politics in the New States," in *Old Societies and New States: The Quest for Modernity in Asia and Africa*, ed. Clifford Geertz (New York: Free Press, 1963).

3. See Paul Brass, "Ethnicity and National Formation," in *Ethnicity* (September 1976), pp. 225–241.

4. Mario Barrera, *Race and Class in the Southwest: A Theory of Racial Inequality* (Notre Dame, Ind.: University of Notre Dame Press, 1979).

5. Alberto Camarillo, *Chicanos in a Changing Society: From Mexican Pueblos to American Barrios in Santa Barbara and Southern California, 1843–1930* (Cambridge, Mass.: Harvard University Press, 1979).

6. See the report of the Subcommittee on Census and Population of the Committee on Post Office and Civil Service, "Problems in Development of the 1980 Census Mail List," Report No. GGD8050, 31 March 1980. See also "Census Data and the Problem of Conceptually Defining the Mexican American Population," *Social Science Quarterly* (March 1973), pp. 661–687; and the Fall 1981 issue of *Daedalus* for a greater explanation of this problem area.

7. See "Mexican Television and Broadcasting Stations," Federal Communications Commission, *Federal Register*, Part V, 11 May 1977; Jorge Reina Schement, "Patterns of Ownership and Employment in Spanish Language Radio Stations of the Southwest," paper presented to the School of Communications, University of Texas, 1977; and Armando Rendon, "Communications and Hispanics: On a New Wave Length," in *Hispanics and Grantmakers*, a special report of the Council of Foundations, Washington, D.C., 1981.

8. Jacques Lafaye, *Quetzalcoatl y Guadalupe* (Mexico City: Fondo de Cultura Economica, 1974). Throughout Latin American countries the same phenomenon is found. In Peru, it is the Virgen Pachamama who appeared to the native Yupanqin; in Ecuador, it is the Virgen Guapulo; and in Paraguay, it is the Virgen Caacupe, for example.

9. On the Catholic Church and Hispanics, see Antonio Stevens Arroyo, ed., *Prophets Denied Honor* (Maryknoll, N.Y.: Orbis Books, 1980), pp. 139–144.

10. Richard Hofstader, *Social Darwinism in American Thought* (Boston: Beacon Press, 1955), pp. 170–200; and Arnoldo De Leon, *They Called Them Greasers* (Austin, Tex.: University of Texas Press, 1983).

11. There are some general histories of the Chicano people. See, for example, Matt S. Meier and Feliciano Rivera, *The Chicanos: A History of Mexican-Americans* (New York: Hill and Wang, 1972) and Rodolfo Acuña, *Occupied America: A History of Chicanos* (New York: Harper and Row, 2d ed., 1981).

12. Jorge Acevedo, "Chicano Thought and Value," in Heydar Reghaby, *Philosophy of the Third World* (Berkeley: Composition, Lewis Publishing, 1974), pp. 129–132.

13. *The Oregonian*, Portland, Oregon, 8 March 1980, p. A-9. The judge did apologize for the remark in open court on the final day of the trial, claiming "Sometimes when you're tired, there's a possibility you might make such statements."

14. See his law review article, "Affirmative Action: A Plea for a Rectification Principle," *Southwestern University Law Review* 9, no. 3 (1977), pp. 597–612.

15. Taped interview of Pedro and Maria Hernandez on 4 December 1971 in Lytle, Texas, by Lydia Serrata. This tape is in the personal collection of materials of this writer deposited with the Mexican-American Library Project of the University of Texas at Austin.

16. Adela Sloss-Vento, *Alonso S. Perales* (San Antonio, Tex.: Artes Graficas, 1977).

17. See Richard Santillan, *La Raza Unida* (Los Angeles, Calif.: Tlaquilo Publications, 1973); Maurilio Vigil, *Chicano Politics* (New York: University Press of America, 1977), pp. 208–219; and Alberto Juarez, "The Emergence of El Partido de la Raza Unida: California's New Chicano Party," *Aztlan—Chicano Journal of the Social Sciences and the Arts*, No. 2 (1972).

18. Taken from remarks given by the commissioner of Immigration and Naturalization Service, Lionel Castillo, at the Centro de Estudios Economicos y Sociales del Tercer Mundo, Mexico City, Mexico, 3–5 October 1980. My own father, Angel Gutierrez Crespo, a political refugee from Mexico in 1928, died in 1958 without renouncing his Mexican citizenship. My grandmother, Refugio Casas de Fuentes, today at age eighty-five refuses U.S. citizenship. She has been in this country since 1914.

19. See the excellent autobiography of Reies Lopez Tijerina, *Mi Lucha por la Tierra* (Mexico City: Fondo de Cultura Economica, 1979).

20. For a legal argument to this claim by Tijerina, see Manuel Ruiz, Jr., *Mexican American Legal Heritage in the Southwest*, a book published by the author in Los Angeles in 1972, registered with the Library of Congress as No. 72–85857.

21. John S. Shockley, *Chicano Revolt in a Texas Town* (Notre Dame, Ind.: University of Notre Dame Press, 1974). See also "The Electoral College and the Mexican American: An Analysis of the Mexican American Impact on the 1972 Presidential Election," prepared by the League of United Latin American Citizens, the Mexican American Bar Association, and the American G.I. Forum, January 1972, for the first written conceptualization of the balance of power potential of the Chicano vote. For a discussion of the role of Chicano students and La Raza Unida Party, see Carlos Muñoz and Mario Barrera's "La Raza Unida Party and the Chicano Student Movement in California," *Social Science Journal* 19 (April 1982), pp. 101–119.

22. Chicanos are still far behind in obtaining a proportionate share of philanthropic monies. See *Hispanics and Grantmakers*, a special report

of the Council on Foundations (Washington, D.C., 1981); and Eugene C. Hill, "Hispanics and Philanthropy," in *The State of Hispanic America*, a publication of the National Hispanic Center for Advanced Studies and Policy Analysis, Oakland, California, 1981.

8

Conclusion

During the 1960s and early 1970s, Mexican-Americans joined blacks, women, and other disadvantaged groups in demanding their share of the American Dream. Just as Martin Luther King, Jr., Stokely Carmichael, and other black leaders were skillful speakers who proclaimed their cause, Mexican-American leaders emerged to articulate the frustrations and demands of many of their people. The four most prominent Chicano leaders were unusually well prepared for such advocacy.

Reies Tijerina and Cesar Chavez shared parallel experiences and common beliefs which were crucial to their respective rhetorical successes. Both began campaigns without personal wealth, political influence, or formal education, yet each could identify with his audiences and had extensive practice in practical public speaking—Tijerina as an itinerant preacher and Chavez as a CSO organizer. Building their confidence in their discourse, both viewed themselves as rhetorical agents in a divine plan destined to be triumphant. Thus, if they presented their messages persistently, they could be assured of success despite obstacles and temporary and temporal setbacks.

Their assurance and skills prepared them well for the ripe, and at the same time discouraging, rhetorical situations they initially encountered.[1] These situations contained the necessary ingredients for rhetorical persuasion: people carrying inchoate resentment, shared dissatisfaction, and acute frustration over immediate exigencies and ongoing conditions. The rhetorical situations facing Tijerina and Chavez might have repelled spokesmen with less faith in words and would likely have decayed without a suitable response. The fittingness of the responses of Chavez and Tijerina included a willingness to orate incessantly. This willingness rested largely on their views of the nature and function of public address.

Rodolfo "Corky" Gonzales and Jose Angel Gutierrez also possessed the experience and skill to be successful spokesmen. Gonzales had given many after-dinner speeches, projected a persuasive persona for barrio youth, and drew examples and ideas from both his urban and rural life. Gutierrez received in-depth training in high school debate and public speaking and studied mass movements in college. Both men were schooled in political leadership and speaking—Gonzales through his participation in the Democratic party, and Gutierrez as a high school student body president and then as a youthful campaigner for local politicians. Ethnic bigotry scarred them both, leaving them with an angry bitterness that translated into intense language and a commitment to speak out.

All four spokesmen relied on their extensive and effective public discourse to gain power and popularity. Their oratorical skills and their commitment to public address were necessary for them to assume leadership and to build their respective organizations. Yet they were far from rhetorical carbon copies.

Chavez spoke calmly and quietly, trusting his clear form, lucid style, and abundant facts to communicate his powerful moral truths. He appeared to be a reasonable teacher, eschewing inflammatory attacks and downplaying his own role in the farm-worker and civil rights movements. Tijerina reflected his evangelist's training and responded to his audience's desire for a millennial savior through his incandescent style and energetic delivery. Like Chavez, he presented many facts, promised that justice would surely prevail, and urged listeners to become active persuaders. While Tijerina focused on the evil of Anglos and later on the promise of the new breed, Chavez stressed human brotherhood and non-violent action. Both appealed to family, God, land, and manliness—values held dear by conservative and close-knit families of migrant workers and rural New Mexicans. Both had faith in legal remedies and evidence, but Tijerina reflected his audience's emphasis on the Spanish heritage by employing symbols of royalty while Chavez endeared himself to Anglos by promoting the brotherhood of all humans.

Gonzales addressed urban barrio youth in the inspirational language of youthful idealism. He vividly portrayed the Anglo as the cause of the Chicano's various problems, and he promoted a cultural nationalism based on the Chicano's heritage and culture in order to harness the political potential of the group and eventually separate and elevate the race. Gutierrez also used vivid language to lay out the case that the Anglo system oppressed Chicanos and that Chicanos must form a third party which would end discrimination and preserve their way of life. Like Gonzales, Gutierrez depicted Chicano youth as the primary agent for change; unlike Gonzales, he sought pragmatic and particular goals, focusing on local political campaigns and a national party more than on a new nation. Both men redefined Mexican-Americans by renaming them, placing as central the race's superior heritage and culture and indicting Anglos for creating the Mexican-Americans' negative self-image. While a major part of Gonzales's impact was through his poem and formal documents, Gutierrez communicated primarily through day-to-day political speaking and a written handbook.

The differences in the public address of the four leaders reflected their different backgrounds, audiences, and goals. Chavez acted out the role of union organizer in the will of God for a millennial betterment of humans. Tijerina was a God-inspired ex-preacher who sought justice and land for unfairly treated and mostly middle-aged northern New Mexican Hispanos. An uncompromising and defiant ex-boxer and successful member of the Establishment, Gonzales drew on his own experiences to explain to young people the evils of the Anglo system and the political road to a new Chicano nation. Gutierrez relied on his college studies and local experiences with political organizing to develop a means to end the discrimination that had seared him.

Together their words created a broad rhetorical vision encompassing the Chicano's past, present, and future. In this vision Anglos caused the material and spiritual problems of Mexican-

Americans, most notably by stealing their land, providing inadequate education, suppressing or co-opting their political efforts, and denying them their history, culture, and language.
Because of this oppression, Chicanos lacked a positive self-identity as well as schooling, jobs, political power, material prosperity, and a culture of their own. The present, however, held
promise of a brighter future, but only if Chicanos learned the
facts of their case, presented it widely, and organized politically.
They had the ingredients of rhetorical as well as political success:
an admirable heritage, culture, and character; and the moral
basis as well as the practical voting power to create change. The
new Chicanos required a new image, a new definition, with
Chicano, Aztlan, and Hispano among the new popular terms
that expressed their pride in being brown.

The new vision contrasted in some ways with that articulated
by Mexican-American moderates, whose major spokesman was
Henry Gonzalez. He, too, was well trained in public address;
he was a skilled speaker whose substantial literary background
surfaced in eloquent addresses. Acknowledging the severe discrimination against his people, he nevertheless argued that hard
work within the established system had led and would continue
to lead to considerable progress. The separatist rhetoric and devil
terms of Gutierrez, he insisted, represented faulty black-and-
white reasoning which stamped its adherents as no better than
white racists. While attacking militants for specific acts and referring to his own life in order to prove that Mexican-Americans
could attain success, he agreed with the militants that the Mexican-American culture must be protected and that education was
central to righting the wrongs against Chicanos.

This study opens a window to the workings of Chicano rhetoric as well as to the vision it communicated. Mexican-Americans
have traditionally given great importance to oral communication
and have responded favorably to diverse rhetorical characteristics and qualities. Respective audiences were persuaded by
various modes of delivery, media of discourse, and themes and
arguments on local issues. Yet it was also true that their common
culture, heritage, language, and experiences produced common
expectations of and responses to rhetorical discourse. As Stan
Steiner has pointed out, barrio leadership has a "unique style,"

and Chicano leaders and spokesmen must reflect particular characteristics, for example, manliness, to be effective.[2] Appeals to family, community, heritage, manhood, God, and oppression by Anglos were particularly potent, and conventionally powerful forms and patterns such as *dichos*, folksayings, anecdotes, *cuentos*, and Spanish formality and graciousness were all potentially effective. These characteristics and qualities could be linked to the rhetorical conventions and cultures of Spain and Mexico and to the Chicano experiences in the United States. It is noteworthy that in the several years of free speech immediately preceding the Spanish Civil War and then during the war itself, most of the leaders of the various political parties were superb orators.[3] Skillful political speaking was apparently prerequisite to leadership in free Spain, just as it has been in Chicano America. In Spanish-speaking or Spanish-influenced cultures, eloquence may be necessary for leadership.

The Chicano leaders inhabited a rhetorical world, believing that effectively employed words on behalf of a just cause had the power to change people and events and that, consequently, Mexican-Americans had the means to improve the established order. The Mexican-American audience was also part of this rhetorical world, expecting and responding to the eloquence of its leaders. The Chicano leaders were not simply swept into leadership by a chain of historical events and ideas that automatically brought forth able spokespersons. Without their impressive ability in public address and the beliefs and attitudes that contributed to their success as orators and writers, they could never have emerged as leaders in the Chicano movement.

The discourse of the four leaders exerted influence far beyond their immediate audiences and organizations. Identifying Tijerina, Chavez, and Gonzales as three outstanding leaders, Ellwyn R. Stoddard points out that the animating ideology of "chicanismo was heavily influenced in its direction and tactics by strong, charismatic leaders."[4] Meier and Rivera note that "little had been done to form national organizations, and few leaders with national exposure had appeared" prior to the early 1960s.[5] They add that "in recent years, however, activist spokesmen of prominence have arisen" and that "four of these young leaders have had considerable impact"—Chavez, Tijerina, Gonzales, and Gutierrez.[6] Knowlton cites the charismatic campaigns of Chavez and Tijerina as a major cause of the entire Chicano protest; and Tony Castro claims that Chavez's movement "opened the door for an outrage that had been pent up for years" in Mexican-Americans.[7]

The spokesmen's influence was sometimes obvious and on other occasions indirect. Author and activist David F. Gomez recalled that his reading of Gonzales's *Yo Soy Joaquin* "reinforced more than anything else I'd read my own growing awareness and feeling of solidarity with him and with our entire *raza*."[8] The quasi-military Brown Berets, who once had chapters in twenty-eight cities, looked to Gonzales and Tijerina for leadership, and especially for ideas on cultural nationalism and ethnic separation.[9] The new ideology of Chicanismo contributed to the founding and motivation of many new organizations, including such campus groups as MECHA (Movimiento Estudiantil Chicano de Aztlan), UMAS (United Mexican-American Students), and MASC (Mexican-American Student Confederation).[10] In politics, Gutierrez's La Raza Unida party elected fifteen candidates in Texas elections in 1962, including two mayors.[11]

The spokesmen were models and catalysts for a new militancy that swept across Mexican America. Professor Marvin Alisky contrasts the "new breed of Mexican-American leader" who spoke frankly with specific evidence and "the old style Mexican-American politician, whose generalities and quiet behavior endeared him to party officials as a reliable source of bloc votes."[12] The national president of the formerly conservative LULAC announced: "The patient attitude of the Mexican-American has ceased. We've gone along with that method for a long time, but it hasn't done us any good. We're fed up with being the stepchildren of the Great Society."[13] The activism peaked with two events in east Los Angeles in 1970. The National Chicano Moratorium Day Committee organized about 25,000 people to protest the disproportionate number of Mexican-Americans being killed in the Vietnam War, and some 600 delegates representing almost all Chicano elements and groups met to work for unity. Protests even shook the venerable foundations of the Catholic Church; a reported 300 "Catolicos por la Raza" disrupted a

Christmas Eve Mass in order to publicize the Church's lack of concern for its people.[14]

In 1966 all Americans learned of the new militance of Mexican-Americans. Feature articles on them appeared for the first time in *Newsweek* (23 May), *Time* (28 April), *U.S. News and World Report* (6 June), and the *Wall Street Journal* (3 May). "In little more than a year, or so it seems" *Newsweek* declared, "the U.S. has awakened to the presence of the American Latin. . . . This hitherto silent 5 percent of the population seems finally on the march toward a new era of genuine political activity."[15] It was the Chicano leadership headed by Gonzales, Tijerina, and Chavez, Maurilio Vigil believes, which "dramatically focused attention on the formerly 'forgotten' minority."[16] This focus was intensified by a rhetorical campaign which expanded beyond the four leaders and beyond public speaking. For example, El Teatro Campesino, a traveling theatrical group, dramatized the injustices committed against brown farmworkers; Gonzales's important poem *Yo Soy Joaquin* was widely distributed and anthologized; and new literary and academic journals, such as *El Grito, Con Safos, Aztlan: Chicano Journal of the Social Sciences and the Arts*, and *Quinto Sol*, began publication.

The awakening produced some encouraging results, a situation which was in sharp contrast with the previous history of Mexican-Americans who received "little response when they protested their plight."[17] The Ford Foundation donated $2.2 million to create the Mexican-American Legal Defense and Education Fund; President Johnson established the first cabinet-level committee on Mexican-Americans; President Nixon appointed an unprecedentedly high number of Hispanics to offices; and the 1972 Democratic and Republican platforms granted the ethnic group unprecedented concessions. In education, courses in Chicano studies and Chicano professors appeared for the first time on many campuses; more Chicanos entered college and professions than ever before; and Spanish was allowed as a language of instruction in public schools in California. In an effort to make the Chicano past and heritage accessible, the first thorough histories of Mexican-Americans were published. Reviewing the gains from the years of protest, Tony Castro concluded that in the 1970s the Mexican-American occupied "a much better place—with far greater prospects—than he held in the early 1960s."[18]

Although the rhetoric of Chicano leaders led both directly and indirectly to material, educational, and political gains, these limited gains did not substantially change the lives of most Mexican-Americans. A more important change occurred in the identity of Chicanos. Their self-image contained increased pride in their history, heritage, culture, and especially their Indian roots. Although questioning whether this new image would benefit Mexican-Americans, Stoddard agreed with other observers on the new "overwhelming ethnic pride" which infused the militant Chicano's identity.[19] In *Newsweek*'s opinion, the stereotype of the listless and sulking Mexican-American had been replaced by a "new Mexican-American militancy. . . . Brown has become aggressively beautiful. And the name of the game is pride and power."[20] Whatever negative features remained in the self-concept were attributed to Anglo oppression rather than to anything inherent in Mexican-Americans.

If Mexican-American problems resulted from discrimination based on color and race, then no legislation could change the biological basis for that discrimination. Instead, the view of their race must be changed. This change first required a new self-identity, a rhetorical redefinition that would form positive pictures in the minds of Anglos as well as Mexican-Americans. Chicano rhetoric was the central tool for this redefinition.

The individual's new self-concept accompanied a growing unity in the community and the entire ethnic group.[21] At the core of this collective unity was Chicano nationalism. The most militant nationalists sought complete control of their communities and dreamed ultimately of a separate state of Aztlan; the more conservative majority became increasingly distrustful of the white-run system but continued to work through that system. In either case, by the 1970s Mexican-Americans were less likely to abandon their ethnic identity and more interested in keeping their heritage, history, and language.

In the early 1970s the Chicano movement and its rhetoric lost intensity, damaged by too many different factions, too many diverse methods, no central organization, and other problems.[22]

To some, the waning anti-Establishment rhetoric indicated that Mexican-Americans had "firmly established a positive group identity" and hence no longer felt threatened by stereotypes.[23] Others thought the revolutionary rhetoric had failed because it did not lead to revolutionary action.[24] To a small group of others, the future required a Marxist defeat of capitalism rather than a commitment to Chicano nationalism.[25] Whatever the future held for Mexican-Americans, Chavez, Tijerina, Gutierrez, and Gonzales had influenced their audiences in ways that could not be undone. As David F. Gomez concluded: "The Chicano movement has brought too many of us together, and we have become too strong to be completely silenced or dismissed."[26]

NOTES

1. For a thorough explanation of rhetorical situations, see Lloyd F. Bitzer, "The Rhetorical Situation," *Philosophy and Rhetoric* 1 (1968), pp. 1–14.

2. Stan Steiner, *La Raza: The Mexican Americans* (New York: Harper and Row, 1969), pp. 192–195.

3. Hugh Thomas, *The Spanish Civil War*, rev. ed. (New York: Harper and Row, 1977), p. 931. This lengthy and authoritative work on the Civil War cites many examples of eloquent speeches and speakers.

4. Ellwyn R. Stoddard, *Mexican Americans* (New York: Random House, 1973), p. 195.

5. Matt S. Meier and Feliciano Rivera, *The Chicanos: A History of Mexican-Americans* (New York: Hill and Wang, 1972), p. 258.

6. Ibid.

7. Clark S. Knowlton, "The Neglected Chapters in Mexican-American History," in *Mexican Americans Tomorrow*, ed. Gus Tyler (Albuquerque: University of New Mexico Press, 1975), p. 46; Tony Castro, *Chicano Power: The Emergence of Mexican America* (New York: Saturday Review Press, 1974), p. 18.

8. David F. Gomez, *Somos Chicanos: Strangers in Our Own Land* (Boston: Beacon Press, 1973), p. 23.

9. Ruth S. Lamb, *Mexican Americans: Sons of the Southwest* (Claremont: Ocelot Press, 1970), p. 125.

10. Meier and Rivera, pp. 250–251.

11. Alberto Juarez, "The Emergence of El Partido de la Raza Unida: California's New Chicano Party," *Aztlan: Chicano Journal of the Social Sciences and the Arts* 3 (Fall 1972), p. 190.

12. Marvin Alisky, "The Mexican-Americans Make Themselves Heard," *The Reporter*, 9 February 1967, p. 45.

13. Quoted in ibid., p. 48.

14. Y. Arturo Cabrera, *Emerging Faces: The Mexican-Americans* (Dubuque, Iowa: William C. Brown, 1971), p. 51.

15. "U.S. Latins on the March," 23 May 1966, p. 32.

16. Maurilio Vigil, *Chicano Politics* (Washington, D.C.: University Press, 1978), p. 252.

17. Castro, p. 18.

18. Ibid., p. 217.

19. Stoddard, pp. 65–70 and 206.

20. "Tio Taco Is Dead," 29 June 1970, p. 22.

21. U.S. Commission on Civil Rights, *The Mexican American* (Washington, D.C.: U.S. Government Printing Office, 1968), p. 2; Meier and Rivera, p. 254.

22. Reasons for the loss of intensity and effectiveness are considered in Armando G. Navarro, "The Evolution of Chicano Politics," *Aztlan: Chicano Journal of the Social Sciences and the Arts* 5 (Spring and Fall 1974), pp. 78–80.

23. Stoddard, p. 225.

24. Navarro, p. 81.

25. Tomas Almaguer, "Historical Notes on Chicano Oppression: The Dialectics of Racial and Class Domination in North America," *Aztlan: Chicano Journal of the Social Sciences and the Arts* 5 (Spring and Fall 1974), pp. 27–54.

26. Gomez, p. xix.

Bibliographic Essay

Speechmaking and other forms of persuasive discourse undeniably played a central role in the Chicano movement. Yet while the rhetorical efforts of blacks during the period of protest have brought forth a number of scholarly book-length studies and scores of articles, Chicano discourse has stimulated little intellectual inquiry. The small yield includes John C. Hammerback and Richard J. Jensen's articles on the "rhetorical worlds" of Cesar Chavez and Reies Tijerina and on the rhetorical strategies of Jose Angel Gutierrez in the *Western Journal of Speech Communication*, Summer 1980; their articles on Rodolfo Gonzales, *WJSC*, Winter 1982, and on Henry B. Gonzalez, *Texas Speech Communication Journal*, 1982; a broad introductory examination by Lloyd D. Powers, "Chicano Rhetoric: Some Basic Concepts," *Southern Speech Communication Journal*, Summer 1973; and Michael Victor Sedano's consideration of the themes of Chicano poetry, *WJSC*, Summer 1980. Added insights into Chicano discourse can be gleaned from varied sources, including a superb, albeit brief, comparison and explication of communication styles and patterns among Mexicans and Americans by John Condon, in *The Bridge*, Spring 1980; interviews with Bert Corona and Jose Angel Gutierrez who share their experiences and viewpoints on Chicano rhetorical discourse, *WJSC*, Summer 1980; and an unpublished paper by Joseph E. Samora, Jr., "Rhetorica al Estilo Chicano: Some Basic Concepts from a Chicano's Viewpoint," presented at the Western Speech Communication Association's annual convention, Phoenix, November 1977. A compilation of many of the articles cited above is Robert W. Mullen's *Hispanic Voices* (Lexington, Mass.: Ginn Publishing, 1984).

Collections of more than a few speeches by Mexican-American leaders are non-existent. Robert Tice's unpublished manuscript, "Rhetoric of La Raza," Chicano Studies Collection, Arizona State University, includes several speech texts. Of the many anthologies that print an occasional speech or piece of written persuasion, probably the most helpful is Matt S. Meier and Feliciano Rivera's *Readings on La Raza: The Twentieth Century* (New York: Hill and Wang, 1974).

During the 1960s and early 1970s, Chicanos contributed novels, plays, poems, and radio and television programs which often had a persuasive or rhetorical dimension. To gain insight into these modes of communication, see Joseph Sommers and Tomas Ybarra-Frausto, *Modern Chicano Writers: A Collection of Critical Essays* (Englewood Cliffs, N.J.: Prentice-Hall, 1979); Roberto J. Garza, *Contemporary Chicano Theatre* (Notre Dame, Ind.: University of Notre Dame Press, 1977); and Francisco J. Lewels, Jr., *The Uses of the Media by the Chicano Movement* (New York: Praeger, 1974).

Assistance for our study has come from scattered scholarly and popular sources. The histories of the Chicano movement have been essential. The most authoritative, Matt S. Meier and Feliciano Rivera's *The Chicanos: A History of Mexican-Americans* (New York: Hill and Wang, 1972), presents vital background and historical context, recognizes the critical place of rhetorical discourse in the movement, and describes the contributions of each of the major Chicano leaders. Rodolfo Acuña's *Occupied America: The Chicano's Struggle Toward Liberation* (San Francisco: Canfield Press, 1972) alters its interpretation somewhat from first to second editions but remains valuable to any study of the movement, its rhetorical discourse, and its leaders. Of the other books on Chicanos, especially helpful are journalist Tony Castro's *Chicano Power: The Emergence of Mexican America* (New York: Saturday Review Press, 1974); Professor Y. Arturo Cabrera's *Emerging Faces: The Mexican-Americans* (Dubuque, Iowa: William C. Brown, 1971); sociologist Joan W. Moore's *Mexican Americans* (Englewood Cliffs, N.J.: Prentice-Hall, 1970); and activist David J. Gomez's *Somos Chicanos: Strangers in Our Own Land* (Boston: Beacon Press, 1973). Stan Steiner's *La Raza: The Mexican Americans* (New York: Harper and Row, 1970) vividly depicts the speaking styles and effects of several Chicano leaders; and Clarke Newlon's *Famous Mexican-Americans* (New York: Dodd, Mead, and Co., 1972), intended for young readers, has brief chapters on many Mexican-American leaders. Two works published too late for consideration in this book will assist in future studies of Chicano discourse: Matt S. Meier's *Bibliography of Mexican American History* (Westport, Conn.: Greenwood Press, 1984), by far the most comprehensive bibliography available; and John R. Chavez's *The Lost Land: The Chicano Image of the Southwest* (Albuquerque: University of New Mexico Press, 1984), which provides an excellent overview of the movement and its leaders.

Helpful essays abound, often in anthologies that gather together vital primary documents as well as insightful interpretive chapters. Among the most useful anthologies are Luis Valdez and Stan Steiner's *Aztlan: An Anthology of Mexican-American Literature* (New York: Alfred A. Knopf, 1972); and Edward Simmen's *Pain and Promise: The Chicano Today* (New York: Mentor Books, 1972). Excellent on the political thoughts of Chicanos is F. Chris Garcia and Rudolph O. de la Garza's *Chicano Politics: Three Perspectives* (North Scituate, Mass.: Duxbury Press, 1977). *Aztlan: Chicano Journal of the Social Sciences and the Arts*, a journal published at UCLA, carries many useful articles, including one by Jose E. Limon (Fall 1973), "Stereotyping and Chicano Resistance: An Historical Dimension," and three in the Spring/Fall 1974 issue which provide provocative viewpoints on Chicano politics: Armando G. Gutierrez and Herbert Hirsch, "Political Maturation and Political Awareness: The Case of the Crystal City Chicano"; Armando Navarro, "The Evolution of Chicano Politics"; and Tomas Almaguer, "Historical Notes on Chicano Oppression: The Dialectics of Racial and Class Domination in North America." A good source of information on the feelings, thoughts, and experiences of Chicano activists is in the Chicano newspapers such as *Con Safos*, the San Bernardino *El Chicano*, and Berkeley's *La Voz del Pueblo*.

Cesar Chavez is the most chronicled Chicano leader. Three of the best of the many books on the man and his farmworker movement are Jacques Levy, *Cesar Chavez: Autobiography of La Causa* (New York: W. W. Norton and Co., 1975); Peter Matthiessen, *Sal Si Puedes: Cesar Chavez and the New American Revolution* (New York: Random House, 1969); and Mark Day, *Forty Acres: Cesar Chavez and the Farm Workers* (New York: Praeger, 1971). Winthrop Yinger's converted M.A. thesis from Fresno State University, *Cesar Chavez: The Rhetoric of Nonviolence* (Hicksville, N.Y.: Exposition Press, 1975), extensively details Chavez's speaking manner and thoroughly analyzes his speech at the end of his twenty-five day fast. Interviews with or articles by Chavez are crucial to determining his view of rhetorical discourse and his experiences as a speaker; among the best are those in *Look* magazine, 1 April 1969, and in the *Christian Century*, 18 February 1970. Brief descriptions of his speeches are in issues of *El Malcriado*, the farmworkers' newspaper. His speeches and essays appear in several anthologies, including that of Meier and Rivera, *Readings on La Raza: The Twentieth Century*. A variety of resources on him and his movement, including texts of his speeches before U.S. government agencies, are in the San Joaquin Valley Farm Workers Collection, Special Collections Department, Fresno State University Library. We also used audiotapes of his speeches housed in the Latin American Library, Oakland Public Library, Oakland, California, in the possession of Chaplain Winthrop Yinger, California Maritime Academy, Vallejo, California, and at the San Jose City College Library; and texts of his speeches provided by Meier and in the book by Tice. Speeches by Chavez located in the Labor History Archives at Wayne State University were not made available to the authors at the time of our writing. Reactions to Chavez's speeches add to our understanding of his rhetorical wizardry and effects, and are scattered in various newspapers, magazines, journals, and books cited in our notes. One of the best is that by Luis Valdez in *Ramparts*, July 1966.

The four biographies on Tijerina offer generous portions and lengthy descriptions of his speeches as well as necessary information on his early background and later prominence. Each author observed the fiery "El Tigre" at first hand. Richard Gardner's *¡Grito! Reies Tijerina and the New Mexico Land Grant War of 1967* (Indianapolis: Bobbs-Merrill, 1970) and Peter Nabokov's *Tijerina and the Courthouse Raid* (Albuquerque: University of New Mexico Press, 1969) are the most detailed. Patricia Bell Blawis's *Tijerina and the Land Grants* (New York: International Publishers, 1971) gives a left-wing activist's version; and Michael Jenkinson's *Tijerina* (Albuquerque: Paisano Press, 1968) offers a more impressionistic account. Nancie Gonzalez, *The Spanish-Americans of New Mexico*, rev. ed. (Albuquerque: University of New Mexico Press, 1969) applies scholarly standards while laying out the context for the Alianza movement and an excellent summary of several interpretations of it. Professor Gordon R. Owen of New Mexico State University contributes a thirty-eight page unpublished manuscript, "Old Activists Never Die—They Just Mellow," which examines Tijerina's speaking and draws from Owen's interviews with Tijerina. Clark S. Knowlton's articles, for example, "The New Mexican Land War," *The Nation*, 17 June 1968; "Tijerina: Hero of the Militants," *The Texas Observer*, 28 March 1969, rest upon the veteran sociologist's extensive study of rural New Mexico. Two indispensable sources are the lengthy taped interviews by Gardner and Jenkinson with Tijerina, in the Peter Nabokov Papers, Zimmerman Library, University of New Mexico; and Tijerina's articles from 1963 to early 1966 in the Albuquerque *News Chieftain*, housed in the Albuquerque Public Library. Tijerina's recollections are also in his *Mi Lucha por la Tierra* (Mexico City: Fondo de la Cultura Economica, 1979). New Mexico newspapers report reactions to Tijerina's speeches; and the Espanola, New Mexico *El Grito del Norte* reveals a militant view of Tijerina and his movement. Hammerback's interviews with Tijerina and with Knowlton, and George W. Grayson, Jr.'s interview with Tijerina in *Commonweal*, July 1967, add important details to Tijerina's story. A film of Tijerina, "The Most Hated Man in New Mexico," NBC Educational Enterprises, captures his intense delivery of speeches.

The most comprehensive book on Rodolfo Gonzales is Christine Marin's *A Spokesman of the Mexican American Movement: Rodolfo "Corky" Gonzales and the Fight for Chicano Liberation, 1966–1972* (San Francisco: R and E Research Associates, 1977). This book also includes primary documents such as Gonzales's widely anthologized "El Plan de Aztlan." Of the numerous articles which detail the events of Gonzales's life, the most useful, "The Poet in the Boxing Ring," first appeared in Steiner's *La Raza: The Mexican Americans.* Less comprehensive essays are in Elizabeth Sutherland Martinez and Enriqueta Longeaux y Vasquez, eds., *Viva La Raza!: The Struggle of the Mexican-American People* (Garden City, N.Y.: Doubleday and Co., 1974); Patty Newman, *Do It Up Brown!* (San Diego: Viewpoint Books, 1971); and Carlos Larralde, *Mexican-American Movements and Leaders* (Los Alamitos, Calif.: Hwong Publishing, 1976). *Yo Soy Joaquin* has been published in English and Spanish by Bantam Books (1972), which added a brief introduction in which Gonzales expresses his views on the poem. The complete text also appears in numerous other sources. Gonzales's other public addresses surface in many collections, including his speeches and written declarations in Valdez and Steiner's *Aztlan: An Anthology of Mexican-American Literature;* Tice; and Meier and Rivera's *Readings on La Raza.* Representative interviews are in *El Grito del Norte,* November 1972; *The Militant,* 17 April 1970; and *La Voz del Pueblo,* May 1971.

The most extensive study of Jose Angel Gutierrez's career is John Staples Shockley's *Chicano Revolt in a Texas Town* (Notre Dame, Ind.: University of Notre Dame Press, 1974). A useful supplement is Calvin Trillin's "U.S. Journal: Crystal City, Texas," *New Yorker,* 17 April 1971. Gutierrez himself has written extensively on the Chicano movement. His most provocative work is *A Gringo Manual on How to Handle Mexicans* (Crystal City, Tex.: Wintergarden Publishing Co., n.d.). His theories on Chicano politics and organizing emerge in *El Politico* (El Paso: Mictla Publications, 1972) and *La Raza and Revolution* (San Francisco: R and E Research Associates, 1972). Also of assistance is his brief diary entitled *The Walkout of 1969: A Diary of Events* (Crystal City, Tex.: Building Trades, 1979). His poem "22 Miles" has been reprinted in several anthologies, for example, in Valdez and Steiner's *Aztlan: An Anthology of Mexican-American Literature.* An essay by Gutierrez on the Chicano movement appears in Alan Rinzler, ed., *Manifesto Addressed to the President of the United States from the Youth of America* (London: Collier-Macmillan Ltd., 1970). Gutierrez's speech, "Mexicanos Need to Control Their Own Destinies," is in *La Raza Unida Party in Texas* (New York: Pathfinder Press, 1971) and in several other books. For a brief essay considering the conflicting arguments of Chicano leaders on the La Raza Unida party, see Robert C. Dick's "La Causa Politica de los Chicanos," *Indiana Speech Journal*, February 1976.

Writings on other Mexican-American leaders active during the period are sparse. The most thorough work is Eugene Rodriguez, Jr.'s biography, *Henry B. Gonzalez: A Political Profile* (New York: Arno Press, 1976). The *Congressional Record* has printed congressional as well as noncongressional speeches by the elected representatives. Gonzalez's persuasive discourse also appears in *The American Federationist*, July 1967, and the *National Elementary Principal*, November 1970. Additional copies are in Valdez and Steiner's *Aztlan: An Anthology of Mexican-American Literature*; F. Chris Garcia, ed., *Chicano Politics: Readings* (New York: MSS Information Corp., 1973); and Livie Isauro Duran and H. Russel Bernard, eds., *Introduction to Chicano Studies*, 2d ed. (New York: Macmillan, 1982). A speech by Senator Montoya, "Woe Unto Those Who Have Ears But Do Not Hear," is in F. Chris Garcia, ed., *La Causa Politica* (Notre Dame, Ind.: University of Notre Dame Press, 1974).

Index

About the Authors

JOHN C. HAMMERBACK is Professor of Speech Communication at California State University, Hayward. He is the editor (with Richard Jensen) of the forthcoming book *In Search of Justice* and has authored or co-authored sixteen articles which appear in the *Quarterly Journal of Speech, Communication Quarterly, Central States Speech Journal, Today's Speech,* and the *Western Journal of Speech Communication.* He is a past president of the Western Speech Communication Association, an associate editor of the *Western Journal of Speech Communication,* and a past chair of the Freedom of Speech Interest Group of WSCA.

RICHARD J. JENSEN is Associate Professor of Speech Communication at the University of New Mexico. He is the editor of the forthcoming *In Search of Justice* (with John C. Hammerback) and *Rhetorical Perspectives on Communications and Mass Media* and has published articles in *Communication Quarterly, Central States Speech Journal,* and the *Western Journal of Speech Communication.*

JOSE ANGEL GUTIERREZ is Associate Professor of Social Sciences at Western Oregon State College. He has written *El Politico, A Gringo Manual on How to Handle Mexicans, Cristal: A Photographic Essay,* and *El Walkout: A Diary of Events.*